MW00795337

Growing the
Fruit of the Spirit

by Larry Kreider & Sam Smucker

House to House Publications
www.h2hp.com

Growing the Fruit of the Spirit

Larry Kreider & Sam Smucker

©2008 by House to House Publications
11 Toll Gate Road, Lititz, Pennsylvania, 17543 USA
Tele: 800.848.5892
www.h2hp.com

ISBN: 978-1-886973-93-0

Printed in the United States of America

Dedication

This book is dedicated to our wonderful wives,
LaVerne Kreider and Sherlyn Smucker,
our partners in life and ministry,
with whom we have journeyed as we experienced
God's principles for healthy living—
growing in the fruit of the Spirit.

Acknowledgments

A very special thanks goes to Karen Ruiz, our editor, Sarah Sauder for cover design and layout, and the teams of leaders, at DOVE Christian Fellowship International and The Worship Center, for giving us the time to write this book and with whom we have been so privileged to serve.

Contents

Growing the Fruit of the Spirit

Introduction

We both have much in common. We grew up as farm boys in Lancaster County, Pennsylvania. I (Sam) grew up Amish and I (Larry) grew up Brethren, both Anabaptists. We both married Mennonite girls. We each had encounters with God as young men after living lives of hypocrisy. We both lived, as young married couples, outside of Pennsylvania for a season, Larry and LaVerne in South Carolina and Sam and Sherlyn in Arizona.

We each began to pastor a new church about 30 years ago in our county in Pennsylvania, before we had ever met. And we have both experienced God's amazing blessing, in spite of ourselves. We have each served for many years as the senior pastor of churches in Lancaster County, and today we both oversee a family of churches and travel nationally and internationally ministering to Christian leaders. We were blessed to start an interdenominational pastor's prayer meeting together over 25 years ago that is still going on today.

We both, furthermore, continue to long for true revival marked by both the power of God and the fruit of God that crosses denominational lines and includes all who call on the name of the Lord. We desire to see his kingdom come and his will to be done on earth as it is in heaven.

During our many years of ministry and Christian leadership, we have met countless persons who told us they were believers in Christ, but their lives seemed spiritually "sluggish." There was something desperately lacking in their lives. Life seemed to be filled with more defeats than victories for them. And it dawned on us that there are so many of God's people who are missing the Bible's nine exercises that are essential for spiritual wellness. These exercise tips for staying fit and healthy spiritually are mentioned in Galatians 5:22-23 and expressed in the believer as growing "the fruit of the Spirit."

This book encourages you to take a spiritual health check of your life. It is a compilation of what we have taught from the scriptures for many years and found to be critical to living a healthy spiritual life and fulfilling our destiny as we bear the fruit of godly Christian character. We believe the message of this book is a clear focus from the heart of God for our generation. Join us on our journey as we experience together God's principles for healthy living—growing the fruit of the Spirit.

Larry Kreider and Sam Smucker
November 2008

Chapter One

Called to Bear Good Fruit

"Remain in me, and I will remain in you. For
a branch cannot produce fruit if it is severed
from the vine, and you cannot be fruitful
unless you remain in me."
John 15:4

You have just met your new neighbor, Jesse, for the
first time. He mentions that he is a semi-professional basketball player. You promptly notice his physique. He is a
short man, quite overweight and lacks any kind of muscle
development. The next day, you glance over at Jesse's
driveway and see him playing basketball with some
friends. He is clumsy and slow and misses every one of
his shots!

It is hard to believe that he is a basketball player. He
does not have the body of a basketball player, he does not
play like a basketball player and he is falling over his own
two feet. A basketball player will bear the fruit of being a
basketball player. He will have a lean body because he

has obeyed the training regimen needed for the sport. He has consumed the right nutrients and practiced persistently so he can propel a ball through a 10 foot high hoop with ease, rarely missing. That is the outcome, or the fruit, of being a basketball player.

Be strengthened spiritually by allowing God to integrate the fruit of the Spirit into your daily spiritual diet and routine!

So many of God's people today are living below their potential and are experiencing defeat on many fronts. They may attend church and claim to be living a Christian life, but the fruit of being a real Christian is hard to find.

As Christians, we must make a decision to respond to God's life within us in order to grow spiritually. And it really does involve making a decision! Just as physical health requires a proactive approach, spiritual vitality and strength comes through allowing God to change us from the inside out.

We go for physical checkups because they are essential to measuring our progress and maintaining our health. Tests for our vision, hearing, cardiac health, and other exams tell our doctor how we are doing physically. We must also assess our spiritual health. We cannot neglect our spiritual health, which is even more important in the long run.

Our body, mind and spirit are connected. There is a vital relationship between them. Whatever affects one will

Growing the Fruit of the Spirit

affect the other. 1 Thessalonians 5:23 seems to bear this out when it makes the connection between body, soul and spirit, "…may your whole spirit and soul and body be kept blameless until our Lord Jesus Christ comes again."

Research shows that taking care of our spiritual health by prayer and meditation can contribute to healing and a sense of well-being in life. Improving our spiritual health may not cure an illness, but it may help us feel better, prevent some health problems and help us cope with illness, stress or death.[1]

Although inter-connected, without a doubt, good spiritual health is infinitely more vital than physical health. No matter how well we care for them, our physical bodies will eventually die, but our spirits will one day receive supernatural bodies that will live for eternity. Understanding the state of our spiritual health is one of the most important things we can do in preparation for that eternal life.

Adding fruit to your spiritual diet

What do we need in order to maintain a high-quality level of spiritual health? We believe the Great Physician's "PDR" (physician's desk reference), otherwise known as the Bible, holds the answers in Galatians 5:22-23.

The Bible gives us nine qualities or virtues that are produced by the action of the Holy Spirit in us, called growing the "fruit of the Spirit." It is fruit that accompanies living a healthy, fulfilled Christian life. You can be strengthened spiritually by allowing God to integrate the fruit of the Spirit into your daily spiritual diet and routine!

The fruit of the Spirit grows as you, by faith, obey God's Word through the guidance and power of God's Spirit. Exactly what kind of fruit growing does God expect from you? Galatians 5:22-23 describes nine attributes that should be visible and plentiful in your Christian life: "But the Holy Spirit produces this kind of fruit in our lives: love, joy, peace, patience, kindness, goodness, faithfulness, gentleness, and self-control...."

The fruit of the Spirit...is an outgrowth of God's nature within.

These are not individual "fruits" from which you pick and choose which ones are the most appealing to you. Rather, the fruit of the Spirit is one nine-fold "fruit" that all Christians should be producing in their lives. The fruit of the Spirit is a manifestation of a life that has been transformed by Jesus Christ.

Spirit fruit is the result of God's life within

These visible traits are a direct result of being filled with God's Spirit and allowing him to work in and through you to make you more like him. Real spiritual fruit is produced only one way. It is formed as the result of God's life within you. Only as real life flows through the branches, does fruit grow. Fruit trees are fed through their roots from the nutrients deep in the soil. Likewise, you need to be deeply rooted and grounded, receiving nourishment from the Vine, Jesus Christ. As you confidently rest or abide in Christ, he gives you the strength necessary to bear fruit that you could not produce on your own.

The fruit of the Spirit cannot be imitated. It cannot be produced by will-power apart from any spiritual life. It is not what a person does, but who he is. Genuine and good fruit (behavior) is the result of a changed heart. It is the result of a heart seeking after God.

"If there's apples on them there branches then that there is an apple tree!"

You immediately know you are looking at an apple tree when you see the ripe apples hanging from its branches. You know without a doubt that it is an apple tree, because apple trees produce apples. It produces what it is.

You've probably heard the saying, "The apple doesn't fall far from the tree." It's often meant that children take after their parents. True Christians will take after their heavenly father. If we are true followers of Christ, we will produce what he is. We bear his genetic code, and have the same traits developing in us that already exist in perfection in him.

"Like" produces "like." Apple trees bear apples. Pear trees produce pears. Blueberry bushes yield blueberries. The kind of fruit which grows on the outside is a reflection of the nature of the tree.

As Christians, our values, perspectives and character will become like God's, because "like produces like." The fruit of the Spirit which grows in your life is an outgrowth of God's nature within. It is the new man, the new life, the new nature growing within you that expresses itself in the kind of fruit that grows on the outside.

In chapter 15 of the Gospel of John, Jesus used a gardening analogy to describe how a Christian will grow and bear spiritual fruit. The visual picture of a vine and a branch symbolizes our identity in relation to Jesus Christ, the Vine. We are likened to a branch on a vine, and we are here on this earth to bear fruit. God compares his people with grapevines that must "produce much fruit" (John 15:5). He expects each of us to produce good and abundant fruit.

God is patient as we develop fruit

How do you cultivate these godly traits in your life and allow them to be developed in you? Fruit does not just one day appear, like magic. It starts as a seed and grows from there. The seeds that cause you to grow are hidden within the fruit of the Spirit.

John Stott, one of the world's leading and faithful Bible teachers says, "If we take care of the seeds, God will take care of the harvest." As you develop the fruit of the Spirit, these seeds grow into fruit and later are scattered and grow into a new tree that can bear more fruit. But it takes time and you must be patient with yourself and others. God is patient with you!

There is a parable in the Bible about a fig tree that did not bear fruit: "Then Jesus told this story: A man planted a fig tree in his garden and came again and again to see if there was any fruit on it, but he was always disappointed. Finally, he said to his gardener, 'I've waited three years, and there hasn't been a single fig! Cut it down. It's just taking up space in the garden.' The gardener answered, 'Sir, give it one more chance. Leave it another year, and I'll give it special attention and plenty of fertilizer. If we get figs next year, fine. If not, then you can cut it down'" (Luke 13:6-9).

"If we take care of the seeds, God will take care of the harvest."

What does this parable tell us? It clearly says that God expects each of us to bear fruit. But it also shows that God will not give up on any of us as long as there is still hope that we will bear fruit. That's extraordinary good news for all of us. God is patient with you as you learn to cultivate the fruit of the Spirit in your life.

In a vineyard, sometimes the branches have a tendency to grow downward along the surface of the ground. There on the ground, the vines get dusty or muddy and they don't get the sunlight or oxygen that is needed to produce fruit. The branches are still connected to the vine, but going their own way.

The gardener desires that they produce fruit. If he cuts them off, he certainly will not get any fruit. Instead, he lifts up the branches, supports them, and washes off the dirty leaves so that the branches will receive the sunlight and oxygen that is needed to produce fruit. This is a beautiful picture of Jesus picking us up out of the dirt, propping us up in love, and cleansing us with the Word.

Fruit trees must be trained and pruned

For those of us who live in a cold winter climate, the long-awaited springtime is a welcomed change. After a long winter, it is refreshing to open the pages of a garden center catalog and see the colorful, luscious fruit that can be grown with a little work on our part. We imagine having trees or bushes in our backyards that produce beautiful fragrant flowers, lush shady foliage and a bountiful harvest of fresh fruit.

But, in order to get to the fruit-bearing stage there are essential things that have to be done in preparation. First of all, the fruit trees must be planted correctly, in the right kind of soil and receiving the appropriate exposure to the sunlight. Periodically applying the right kind of fertilizer and mulch is vital, as well. Even more importantly, fruit trees must be kept properly pruned so they produce bigger and better fruit. Pruning allows the fruit tree to direct nutrients to branches that will bear high quality fruit.

Just as it takes time for fruit to grow until it ripens, you too will find yourself in "growing seasons" in your life where you are being cultivated by God and at times pruned by God so that you can produce good fruit. When

God prunes or cuts those things from your life that pull you away from him, he does it for your own good.

He may want to prune areas of your thought patterns, desires, habits or ways of dealing with certain issues before they overtake you or pull you into sin. That's what this book is all about—learning how you can allow God to produce the fruit of a true Christian life through the power of the Holy Spirit working within you. God knows the beauty of who you can become. He knows that pruning will greatly improve your spiritual health and strength.

We will learn how to allow the Great Gardener to cultivate and prune us so that each of the nine fruit is plentiful in our lives.

As a Christian, we need to examine ourselves routinely for the presence of fruit, for the abundance of fruit and the quality of fruit in our life. Fruit is never meant to be left hanging on the tree to ripen, rot and fall off. Fruit is meant to give life and health to those around you who can see the fruit, and pick it to eat. Through your love, joy, peace, patience, kindness, goodness, faithfulness, gentleness and self-control, you will bless others with the fruit of your Christian life, and through it, bring spiritual life, health and blessing to those around you.

What are you producing from your life?

A Christian walking in close fellowship with God will bear the fruit of the Spirit, just like an apple tree that has been fertilized and cultivated bears delicious apples. But we need to be observant and perceptive.

Some trees bear good fruit and others bear bad fruit. Jesus himself said in Matthew 7:17-20 that "...every good tree bears good fruit, but a bad tree bears bad fruit. A good tree cannot bear bad fruit, and a bad tree cannot bear good fruit. Every tree that does not bear good fruit is cut down and thrown into the fire. Thus, by their fruit you will recognize them." This scripture shows us there are two types of fruit, bad fruit that will destroy us and good fruit that will advance us for God's service and bless many.

What exactly is bad fruit? Bad fruit is acting on the desires of our sinful nature. In Galatians, just two verses before the fruit of the Spirit is mentioned, we see a clear contrast between the life-style of someone who is filled with the Holy Spirit and someone who is controlled by their sinful nature and bears bad fruit.

Galatians 5:19-21 says, "When you follow the desires of your sinful nature, the results are very clear: sexual immorality, impurity, lustful pleasures, idolatry, sorcery, hostility, quarreling, jealousy, outbursts of anger, selfish ambition, dissension, division, envy, drunkenness, wild parties, and other sins like these. Let me tell you again, as I have before, that anyone living that sort of life will not inherit the Kingdom of God" (Galatians 5:19-21).

Each of us "produces" something from our lives. A person's life can produce the fruit of jealousy and selfish ambition or kindness and serving others. It can produce joyfulness and humility or hatred and bitterness. Bearing the right kind of fruit is a crucial part of our spiritual growth. If you want good fruit, you must cultivate the fruit of the Spirit: love, joy, peace, patience, kindness, goodness, faithfulness, gentleness and self-control.

Each of us "produces" something from our lives.

In this book we will learn how to allow the Great Gardener to cultivate and prune us so that each of these nine fruit is plentiful in our lives and of the highest quality. But before we look at these spiritual fruit-growing exercises for healthy living, in the next chapter we are going to see how God takes us through a growing process, in a greenhouse environment (sometimes called a "hothouse"). These training times, where we get special attention, are preparation times for the fruit that will eventually come from our lives as we learn to grow more into the Great Gardener's likeness.

[1] "Spirituality and Health," 2000-2008 American Academy of Family Physicians, http://familydoctor.org/online/famdocen/home/articles/650.html, accessed July 15, 2008.

Fruit for Thought

1. How do you personally make decisions each day to maintain your spiritual health? How are you adding fruit to your spiritual diet?

2. Describe ways you already see the Holy Spirit cultivating the life-transforming qualities of the fruit of the Spirit in your life.

3. How has God been patient with you as you develop the fruit of the Spirit in your life?

Chapter Two

The Greenhouse

"Trials teach us what we are; they dig up the
soil, and let us see what we are made of; they
just turn up some of the ill weeds
on to the surface."

Charles H. Spurgeon

The Japanese bonsai tree can be dwarfed and stunted
by keeping its roots clipped. It is kept miniature through
pot confinement and crown and root pruning and will never
grow to its full size if trained in this way. Although this
millennia-old art form of the miniaturization of trees is
aesthetic and appealing, God does not want you to be like
bonsai trees, stunted with clipped roots!

In fact, scripture tells us otherwise. He wants your
spiritual roots to grow and to go deeper and deeper so you
can produce abundant fruit in your life. Jeremiah 17:7-8
in the Amplified Bible says, "Most blessed is the man
who believes in, trusts in, and relies on the Lord, and whose
hope and confidence the Lord is. For he shall be a like a

tree planted by the waters that spreads out its roots by the river; and it shall not see and fear when heat comes; but its leaf shall be green. It shall not be anxious or full of care in the year of drought, nor shall it cease yielding fruit."

Do you know what that tells you? It tells you that if you allow God to grow you and if you permit your spiritual roots to go deeper and deeper into him, his character will come out and you will yield fruit. No matter what comes, no matter what you encounter—even when the pressure is on—you can continue to demonstrate God's character in your life.

Get special attention in the hothouse

You can be sure that you will find yourself in the hothouse sometimes! In fact, from time to time God allows us all to experience periods in a greenhouse so we can get special attention from him until we gain strength and grow and develop so we are better able to flourish on the outside. He may want to teach you something in order to develop his character in you so that you can eventually bear fruit.

Most of us do not like the greenhouse experience. Hothouses are hot! Sometimes it's hard to breathe in a greenhouse. The sweat drips off our face, our hands get dirty. But greenhouses maintain the proper atmosphere for plants to grow strong so they are prepared for the outside world. It's where God trains you and me to be productive.

My (Larry) parents raise chrysanthemum flowers. They seed and transplant them in the greenhouse first for a couple of months until they grow strong enough to plant outside. You could imagine that for plants, times in a hothouse may not always be pleasant. They are transplanted, cut, pruned, grafted, thinned and weeded. It is hot and humid, and plants dry out quickly and literally get parched until they are watered. Greenhouse workers know that developing healthy plants entails the radical handling of cutting and pruning so they can grow strong enough to make it on the outside.

Times in a hothouse may not always be pleasant.

Jesus understood the importance of pruning both vines and disciples. He said, "I am the true grapevine, and my Father is the gardener. He cuts off every branch of mine that doesn't produce fruit, and he prunes the branches that do bear fruit so they will produce even more. You have already been pruned and purified by the message I have given you. Remain in me, and I will remain in you. For a branch cannot produce fruit if it is severed from the vine, and you cannot be fruitful unless you remain in me. Yes, I am the vine; you are the branches. Those who remain in me, and I in them, will produce much fruit. For apart from me you can do nothing. Anyone who does not remain in me is thrown away like a useless branch and withers. Such branches are gathered into a pile to be burned. But if you remain in me and my words remain in you, you may ask for anything you want, and it will be granted! When you produce much fruit, you are my true disciples. This brings great glory to my Father" (John 15:1-8).

Experience stimulating growth!

It's a little known fact, but a solution for a tree that is not bearing much fruit is to whack the side of its trunk several times with a baseball bat. It sounds crazy, but it works. It does not hurt the tree, but as a living thing it feels like it is under attack, and therefore needs to produce some seeds so the species will carry on after it dies. In essence, it stimulates the tree's reproductive hormones, and the tree goes into survival mode, which helps it to carry on through difficult times.

A similar thing happens when you trim a fruit tree. Drastic pruning of a tree is essential to ensure healthy fruit production. It seems radical, but annual pruning of your fruit tree leads to a healthier tree with a heavier fruit production. By cutting off the old, the new can grow!

Developing holy character involves training exercises

As "branches" we must learn totally to depend on the Vine to produce godly, holy Christian character. Relying on the Vine involves being willing to be trained and pruned because God has called us to be holy and obedient children, and it doesn't happen overnight.

So you must live as God's obedient children. Don't slip back into your old ways of living to satisfy your own desires. You didn't know any better then. But now you must be holy in everything you do, just as God who chose you is holy (1 Peter 1:14-15).

To be holy is to be set apart. Holiness is living a life that is set apart for the purposes of God. God is calling you today to be an individual that fulfills God's purpose as an obedient child.

The Bible says, "For many are called, but few are chosen" (Matthew 22:13-15). What does that mean? God has called all to fulfill his purposes in the kingdom. But only some choose to follow him and are willing to be chosen by the Lord to be trained by him.

There's an old story told about several horses that were corralled so that a horse trainer could train them for a special purpose. After a few days one horse says, "I am sick of this training. It's too hard," and he jumps the fence to freedom.

Before long, all the horses follow suit and jump the fence except for one. That one horse sticks with it to get trained even though it feels excruciating. He endures all the **Drastic pruning of a tree is essential to ensure healthy fruit production.** hard work required of a driving horse—including the bridle with its blinders, noseband, harness, bits and reins. During this training, his old horse buddies occasionally stopped by the corral and related stories of the fun they were having being wild and free. Sometimes the horse couldn't help but think to himself, "Is all this discipline and hard work really worth it?"

Then one day he found out why he was being trained. He was being prepared as the king's personal horse, and soon he was strutting elegantly through the city with the prestigious job of pulling the king's carriage. Before long, his horse friends saw him and wondered, "How did he get *that* job?"

Of course, he had the job because he had gone through the training and persevered. After a short time, a famine came on the land. Since this horse had been trained to pull the king's carriage, all of his needs were met. Plentiful food was provided and he had a warm stable to sleep in. All of the horse's friends who had not been willing to go through the training school, were now starving and dying and complaining. But it was too late for them. They had not been willing to take the time needed to be properly trained by the master.

God has training schools for every one of us, to teach us to walk in holiness, to be set apart for him. He has a unique plan for you and me, but we must first be obedient and learn to walk in holiness.

We must fall in love with Jesus and fall out of love with the world. We must seek his kingdom first and pursue holiness. God is calling you to a new level of holiness, but it may require going through some greenhouses where you are pruned and nurtured so that you become strong spiritually and learn to obey God.

We have both gone through many greenhouse preparation experiences in our lives. Years ago, as a busy young husband in business and also reaching out to youth in the evenings, I (Larry) came to the abrupt realization that my marriage was suffering. We just didn't seem to have the love for each other that we once had. We received marriage counseling, and we came out of the greenhouse stronger and better equipped because God had trained us and called us to a new level of holiness in our marriage. Today, more than three decades later, we are very much in love!

As a young pastor, I (Larry) led an exciting, new, growing church. I remember going to pastors' conferences where pastors would talk about their many problems in leading a church, and I thought to myself, "Wow, we don't have any problems, because we pray about everything...maybe if they would pray more...!" I was proud of our accomplishments, but God deemed it necessary to take me through a greenhouse experience so that I would to-

God has training schools for every one of us, to teach us to walk in holiness, to be set apart for him.

tally and fully lean on him. Several years into this church plant, I came to the place where I felt misunderstood by others.

People began to leave our church including some good leaders. It was one of the hardest times of my life, and I was ready to quit. Thankfully, by the grace of God, it was in this greenhouse experience that I began to realize how much pride I had and repented before the Lord. I found that what mattered was not what I did for God, but that he loved me and I was pleasing to him, just because he loved me; period. God was taking me to a new level of holiness in his greenhouse.

Thriving during the greenhouse experiences

The Bible is filled with examples of those who went through God's greenhouse experiences. Paul went through many greenhouse experiences when he was persecuted by the religious leaders of his day for his faith in Christ. Moses was royalty and served in Pharaoh's courts and God had a clear call on his life—to lead the Israelites out of Egypt. But he attempted to fulfill that call with his own power when he killed an Egyptian. Subsequently, he spent 40 years in a wilderness experience where God further prepared him.

Jesus, himself, went through his heavenly Father's greenhouse. He was God's son, but for his first 30 years he lived with his family and worked in a carpenter's shop, learning the trade of a carpenter. It was hard work, and I'm sure at times monotonous. Even at a young age, he could easily have sat down with the Rabbis and taught them, but God put him in the carpentry shop to learn to work with his hands and do manual labor. In this training time, Jesus learned to do those things a carpenter does well—repair things and build things from scratch. There is a parallel with carpentry and how Jesus repairs lives today and sees our potential even with our flaws and sin. In the carpentry shop Jesus learned how to sand wood when he needed to, and to polish at other times. He learned how to see the potential in a piece of wood just as he sees the potential in you and me today.

Your greenhouse experience today is helping you grow and develop to become more like Jesus.

Joseph went through a long, lonely greenhouse experience, starting as a young boy. His grand dreams about how God would use him were misunderstood, and his brothers thought, "This kid is out to lunch!" You probably know the story. They sold him into slavery, and he ended up in Egypt. In this training place, God tested him time and time again because the call of God was so great on his life. If you're going through some hard times right now, rest assured, God probably has greater things than you can ever imagine in store for you in your future. Your greenhouse experience today is helping you grow and develop to become more like Jesus.

In Joseph's experience, even when he did the right thing and avoided his boss's wife's advances, he was thrown into jail anyway. Again, he had to experience hard times before they got better. Sometimes you may feel you are doing what God wants you to do, and it gets worse. In jail, Joseph persevered. He heard from God and interpreted the dreams of two prison mates. But Joseph was forgotten in jail, even though he had accurately interpreted the dreams of the butler and the baker.

In the timing of the Lord, word got out about this dream-interpreter, and he was brought before the king and properly interpreted the dream that was terrifying him. Then Pharaoh pardoned Joseph and made him second in command of the whole empire of Egypt. Through his greenhouse experiences, Joseph learned to be an obedient child of God.

We're in the greenhouse for a season, not forever

Hebrews 12:5-11 explains how God takes us through greenhouse seasons or times of discipline so we can learn from them:

"And have you forgotten the encouraging words God spoke to you as his children? He said, 'My child, don't make light of the Lord's discipline, and don't give up when he corrects you. For the Lord disciplines those he loves, and he punishes each one he accepts as his child. As you endure this divine discipline, remember that God is treating you as his own children. Who ever heard of a child who is never disciplined by its father? If God doesn't discipline you as he does all of his children, it means that you are illegitimate and are not really his children at all. Since we respected our earthly fathers who disciplined us, shouldn't we submit even more to the discipline of the Father of our spirits, and live forever? For our earthly fathers disciplined us for a few years, doing the best they knew how. But God's discipline is always good for us, so that we might share in his holiness. No discipline is enjoyable while it is happening—it's painful! But afterward there will be a peaceful harvest of right living for those who are trained in this way.'"

The Lord disciplines you so that you may share in his holiness. God is preparing you in holiness for his service! It is not always pleasant, and it may seem like everything is going wrong and nothing is happening. But, if you allow yourself to be trained during the greenhouse experiences, they produce a harvest.

Sometimes we try to place the blame for our season of discipline on the devil. Other times we may think that we did something wrong and God is correcting us. But this may not be the case. There are certainly times when we need to resist the devil, but sometimes we give him too much credit.

> **God takes us through greenhouse seasons or times of discipline so we can learn from them.**

We may be in God's greenhouse simply because he is preparing us for something that is so good it would blow our minds if we knew all of the details about it today. And, remember, plants stay in the greenhouse for a season, not forever.

Gifts are given, but fruit is developed

In the next nine chapters we will take a look at the

Lord's nine exercises for healthy living—the fruit of the Spirit. These are not to be confused with the gifts of the Spirit. Gifts are given to be used, but fruit must be grown.

If we were to give you an appliance or a tool for a birthday gift, it would be free. It is a gift! All you need to do is to use it. But fruit starts out like a seed, and it must be cultivated and fertilized and watered in order to grow.

The supernatural gifts of the Spirit are gifts given to individuals for them to use to magnify God and help other people. 1 Corinthians 12:8-10 lists these nine gifts:

"To one person the Spirit gives the ability to give wise advice; to another the same Spirit gives a message of special knowledge. The same Spirit gives great faith to another, and to someone else the one Spirit gives the gift of healing. He gives one person the power to perform miracles, and another the ability to prophesy. He gives someone else the ability to discern whether a message is from the Spirit of God or from another spirit. Still another person is given the ability to speak in unknown languages, while another is given the ability to interpret what is being said."

The fruit of the Spirit, found in Galatians 5:22-23, includes love, joy, peace, patience, kindness, goodness, faithfulness, gentleness and self-control. These are all the result of God growing his character within us. They come as a seed in each of us and must be matured or exercised.

Bible teacher Joyce Meyer once said, "God told me if I'd put half as much time in developing the fruit of the Spirit as I did in the gifts, I'd already have both. Gifts will get you somewhere but won't give you enough character to keep you there once you get there!" We should not give too much attention to people's gifts without discerning their character or their fruit. Gifts really are not worth too much without developing the fruit. It is from the character (the fruit) of Christ that our gifts will come forth in power.

The fruit of the Spirit is the result of God growing his character within us.

Matthew 7:20 says it best, "Yes, just as you can identify a tree by its fruit, so you can identify people by their actions." Are our actions displaying the fruit of the Spirit?

Let's take a look at the first fruit of the Spirit listed in Galatians 5:22—love. As Christians, our love walk must be developed, first and foremost.

Fruit for Thought

1. Describe a time you were in the "greenhouse." How did you get special attention from God there?

2. How do you develop holy character?

3. What is the difference between the fruit of the Spirit and the gifts of the Spirit?

Chapter Three

Love

"Love is a fruit in season at all times, and
within reach of every hand."
Mother Teresa

From the time Sharon was a little girl, she always de-
sired a relationship with her father, but he was "not avail-
able." He had no time for her, and eventually her heart
gave up. Not that her dad ever noticed. He moved away
and didn't bother to leave a forwarding address.

Years later, on Father's Day, Sharon was reading her
Bible, and had an urgent prompting to call her Dad who
now lived in Florida. She hadn't spoken to him in years.
She telephoned him to wish him a Happy Father's Day
and got the usual response. He was cold and indifferent.
But at that moment, something swept over Sharon—it was
love…suddenly, her Dad's response really didn't matter.
She was free to love him just as he was without expecting
to receive anything in return. Sharon couldn't explain it,

but she knew that the Holy Spirit had deposited love into her spirit so she could supernaturally love her dad, with no expectancy of the love being reciprocated.

This is the first of God's spiritual fruit, produced by the action of the Holy Spirit in you. It is the fruit of "love." The Greek word for this kind of love is "agape." This Greek word translated into English means "love." Not just any kind of love but the love God offers us that says, "I choose to love you with no conditions or expectation of reciprocation." It is unconditional, unwavering and selfless.

God's love is a love that knows no limits. It is giving with no expectancy of return. This love is not based on feelings, but is based on the truth that we are loved by a heavenly father who just loves us because he loves us! 1 John 3:1 tells us: "See how very much our Father loves us, for he calls us his children, and that is what we are!" We love him and others because He loved us first!

God is love

Agape love is the unearned love God has for humanity—a love so great that he was willing to send his only son to suffer and die on our behalf. God fully demonstrated his limitless love to us when he gave his only son who lay down his life at the cross. The Bible says, "There is no greater love than to lay down one's life for one's friends" (John 15:13).

The story is told of five-year-old Mary who underwent a serious operation, had lost considerable blood and needed a transfusion. A test showed that her brother Jimmy's blood matched hers. When the doctor asked Jimmy if he would give his sister some of his blood, Jimmy agreed to it. During the transfusion, the doctor noticed that Jimmy was getting pale for no apparent reason.

God's love is a love that knows no limits.

"Are you feeling ill, Jimmy?" asked the doctor.

"No, sir!" said Jimmy, "but I'm just wondering when I will die."

"Die!" gasped the doctor. "Do you think people die when they give blood to someone else?"

"Yes sir!" replied Jimmy.

"And you were going to give your life for Mary?"

"Yes sir!" replied the boy simply.

"Why?" the doctor asked.

"Because she is my sister and I love her."

Of course this doesn't mean we have to die for others, but we should be prepared to step out of our comfort zone and serve others as we follow his example "not to be served, but to serve." To serve unselfishly, we really have to learn to walk in agape love because agape love is capable of functioning even in a hostile environment during those times there are not warm fuzzy feelings or emotions to back it up. Although love may involve our emotions, it is primarily a commitment to care about others. God desires our love to grow so big that it will chase people down and overtake them with its unselfish, extravagant and servant-like behavior.

Jesus Christ is the expression of perfect love. If we are going to follow his example, we need to lay down our lives for others. 1 John 4:7-8 tells us: "Dear friends, let us continue to love one another, for love comes from God. Anyone who loves is a child of God and knows God. But anyone who does not love does not know God, for God is love."

God is love, and he lives in us. So then, love lives in us! Sometimes we try so hard to produce the fruit of love. Imagine an apple tree trying really hard to produce good apples. This sounds crazy, doesn't it? An apple tree does not try harder to produce apples during times of drought or other adverse conditions, it just goes deeper into the soil and receives water and nutrients, and the fruit grows on its branches. In the same way, as we go deeper into the water of God's word and trust his Holy Spirit to live through us in times of spiritual drought, we produce good fruit!

1 Corinthians 13, the love chapter of the Bible, says it like this: "If I could speak all the languages of earth and of angels, but didn't love others, I would only be a noisy gong or a clanging cymbal. If I had the gift of prophecy, and if I understood all of God's secret plans and possessed all knowledge, and if I had such faith that I could move mountains, but didn't love others, I would be nothing. If I gave everything I have to the poor and even sacrificed my

body, I could boast about it; but if I didn't love others, I would have gained nothing. Love is patient and kind. Love is not jealous or boastful or proud or rude. It does not demand its own way. It is not irritable, and it keeps no record of being wronged. It does not rejoice about injustice but rejoices whenever the truth wins out. Love never gives up, never loses faith, is always hopeful, and endures through every circumstance...love will last forever!" (1 Corinthians 13:1-8).

Love may involve our emotions, but it is primarily a commitment to care about others.

Try placing your name in this scripture every time it mentions love or refers to love and repeating this scripture out loud. For example, if your name is Joan you can say: "Joan is patient, Joan is kind. Joan is not jealous, Joan does not boast, Joan is not proud. Joan is not rude, Joan does not demand her own way, Joan is not irritable, Joan keeps no record of being wronged. Joan does not rejoice about injustice but rejoices when the truth wins."

This is God's plan for us to experience the fruit of his love in our lives. God spoke the universe into existence in Genesis, chapter 1. He said, "Let there be light, and there was light!" And as we speak the truth of God's word we experience his love in our lives. But how can we love when we don't feel very loving?

Love in action

We often think we must feel love. Love is not a feeling, but a decision. And when we make the decision to love, the feelings will follow. David Wilkerson, the founder of Teen Challenge and pastor of Times Square Church in New York City, nearly fifty years ago was a young pastor reaching out to drug addicts in New York City.

He tells the story of a young staff person who came to help him one day. The young lady told David she had no love for the people in the part of the city they were reaching out to. David wrote an address on a piece of paper and gave it to her and told her to go to the address, knock on the door and tell the lady who opened the door that she was there to serve her.

Later that day, the young girl came back to David, beaming. "I now have feelings of love." she said. "After cleaning and serving the mother who opened the door today, I am filled with love and compassion." She simply had to take a step of faith and serve, and God gave her the love she was looking for.

How love grows

God is love, and his nature is love. He wants us to reach out to others with that same limitless love. When we love one another with an *agape* type love, the Spirit of God can work through us in the lives of other people that need to see the love of Jesus.

But how do we grow that Holy Spirit-nourished fruit called love? How do we serve others in love?

The apostle Paul wrote, "...For we know how dearly God loves us, because he has given us the Holy Spirit to fill our hearts with his love" (Romans 5:5). When a Christian receives God's Spirit, he receives the love of God. Over time, through actively exercising it, the depth and amount of love grows.

The Bible tells us that Paul prayed for the Philippian believers that their love would grow and flourish. "So this is my prayer: that your love will flourish and that you will not only love much but well. Learn to love appropriately. You need to use your head and test your feelings so that your love is sincere and intelligent, not sentimental gush. Live a lover's life, circumspect and exemplary, a life Jesus will be proud of: bountiful in fruits from the soul, making Jesus Christ attractive to all, getting everyone involved in the glory and praise of God" (Philippians 1:9 The Message).

Love calls us to each other

As a Christian, as you seek to grow the fruit of the Spirit, especially love, it opens the way to a life of fruitfulness and spiritual productivity. Love is one of the fruit of the Spirit which is the very nature of Jesus being produced within you, and it spills out to those around you.

Love is a fruit given to us by God for us to give away. One night in New York, on Broadway, the great star, Mary

Martin, was preparing to go on stage, as she had a 1,000 times before, in Rodger & Hammerstein's "South Pacific." Just before she took stage a note was handed to her. The letter was signed, Oscar Hammerstein, who was that very evening on his death bed.

"The note was short. It simply said: 'Dear Mary, A bell's not a bell until you ring it. A song's not a song until you sing it. Love in your heart is not put there to stay. Love isn't love till you give it away.'

"When the play was over the cast rushed her backstage and asked, 'What happened? We've never seen you perform that way before?'

"Mary read to them Hammerstein's note and said, 'Tonight, I gave my love away.'"[1]

You can experience love for God and love for people that far exceeds your mere human capability. *Agape* love is a reflection of the fact that God loves you, and is an expression of Christ's love active in you as you reach out to others.

"Love can never be simply between you and God. It can never be limited to that relationship. Jesus makes that clear. Love is more than the relationship between a man and a woman, no matter how extraordinary it may be. Love is ever expanding. Love always grows, not just deeper, but wider. Love always loves people more and always loves more people. Love calls us to community; love calls us to humanity; love calls us to each other." [2]

Growing the Fruit of the Spirit

In Acts 9 we read the account of a lady named Dorcas. There is nothing reported about what she said, only about what she did. She expressed the Spirit fruit of love through her actions. Some of the wonderful deeds that she did in Jesus' name and out of love for him were helping the poor, sewing and giving away clothing to those in need. She gave witness to Jesus by her service to others, and people noticed.

Our actions as Christians testify to the power of God's love working in our lives.

Our actions as Christians testify to the power of God's love working in our lives. Pay attention to others. A kind word, a helpful deed, an unexpected gift are ways that we can let our light shine and our love show. And remember, the Bible says in the last verse of the love chapter: "And now these three remain: faith, hope and love. But the greatest of these is love" (1 Corinthians 13:13). As we learn to grow the spiritual fruit of love and release it to permeate our lives, the other eight fruit will have the groundwork on which to grow and multiply.

[1] SermonCentral.com. http://www.sermoncentral.com/SearchResults30.asp, accessed July 21, 2008.

[2] Erwin Raphael McManus, *Soul Cravings, Intimacy: Entry 16,* (Nashville, TN: Thomas Nelson Inc., 2006).

Fruit for Thought

1. Describe a time you loved even though you didn't feel very loving. What kind of love was this?

2. How is love a decision, not a feeling?

3. How tender is your heart toward God and toward other people? How have you loved others beyond your human capability?

Chapter Four

Joy

"Joy is the holy fire that keeps our purpose
warm and our intelligence aglow."
Helen Keller

You only have to observe a group of young children at play, with their spontaneous and uninhibited antics, to learn the meaning of the word "joy." When children are happy they show it. They greet the world with a sense of wonder and delight. The fruit of joy is the second of God's visible traits that are produced by the Holy Spirit within you, resulting in getting spiritually fit and healthy.

The dictionary tells us that *joy* is *a cheerfulness or a calm delight.* Joy is a deep well on the inside of us, an inward reality which produces an outward radiance. It is an orientation of the heart. It is a settled state of contentment, assurance and hope. And most important of all, joy is unaffected by circumstances.

In 1974, I (Sam) experienced a tragedy that no parent should ever have to face. Our young son was killed in a traffic accident. For the first couple of days I was in shock and felt intense and overwhelming despair. Finally, I said to my wife Sherlyn, "Hon, this is too hard. I'm not sure we will survive this grief, but we must make a choice. We are going to stand up and worship God even though it seems impossible."

It was not easy. But as we praised the Lord, things turned around; our despair turned to hope, and our hope turned to joy. We learned, firsthand, that joy is a fruit of the Spirit, not a fruit of our circumstances.

Joy changes our spiritual climate

In the Bible, we notice that joy and worshiping God often go hand-in-hand, resulting in a "climate-change" in our circumstances or in the way we perceive them.

A single characteristic of Jewish worship was great joy. In fact, the reputation of joy had so spread that when the Babylonians captured Israel they taunted them by saying, "Sing us one of the joyful songs of your country." The Book of Acts talks about people being filled with joy and the Holy Ghost. The redeemed made melody in their hearts. After the Samaritan city received salvation, "There was great joy in the city." Paul says without apology, "The Kingdom of God is not meat and drink but righteousness, and peace, and joy in the Holy Ghost" (Romans 14:17).[1]

Not too long ago, I (Larry) had the privilege of speaking at a Christian Leadership Convention in the nation of Rwanda. We visited the Genocide Museum in Kigali, the capital city, and although I knew about the terrible genocide in their nation, I was unprepared to come face to face with one of the worst tragedies in all of history when over one million people from one tribe were slaughtered by their tribal neighbors within three months in 1994. My African friends who invited me to Rwanda had been in exile in neighboring Congo during the killings. They came home after the genocide to find their family members murdered and hundreds of thousands of orphans in the land.

Notice that joy and worshiping God often go hand-in-hand, resulting in a "climate-change" in our circumstances.

They had to face the hard question, could they forgive those who had so ruthlessly murdered their loved ones? They chose to give praise to God regardless of the circumstances they faced, and God gave them the grace to forgive.

Today these Christians are active in reaching out to those around them with the love of Jesus. They are even going into the prisons and telling those who killed their loved ones that they have forgiven them, and sharing with them the good news of the gospel of Jesus Christ. They are joyful Christians who have encountered adverse circumstances and overcome.

Jesus is a joy bringer

I (Sam) remember as a little boy not being allowed to crack a smile in church. There was very little, if any, joy when I attended church services, and I grew up thinking Jesus must be a very serious, somewhat depressed God. Too often Jesus is depicted this way—as a solemn, melancholic ascetic.

A closer examination of scripture reveals that Jesus came as a joy giver—a joy bringer who lived in the fullness of life that comes with living one hundred percent in the Father's will one hundred percent of the time. He came to show us what God was really like. Scripture tells us that even from the very beginning of time, Jesus rejoiced in the presence of a joyful God:

"The Lord formed me from the beginning, before he created anything else. I was appointed in ages past, at the very first, before the earth began. I was born before the oceans were created, the springs bubbled forth their waters. Before the mountains were formed, before the hills, I was born—before he had made the earth and fields and the first handfuls of soil. I was there when he established the heavens, when he drew the horizon on the oceans. I was there when he set the clouds above, when he established springs deep in the earth. I was there when he set the limits of the seas, so they would not spread beyond their boundaries. And when he marked off the earth's foundations, I was the architect at his side. *I was his constant delight, rejoicing always in his presence.* And how happy I was with the world he created; how I rejoiced with the human family!" (Proverbs 8:22-31).

I don't believe that most of the pictures of Jesus we have are really accurate. I think he smiled and had a lot of fun and exuded joy. Certainly he was sad at times. The Bible tells us he was a man acquainted with sorrows and grief. He understands our weaknesses and was tested in every way that we are tested.

He wept with those who wept, he rejoiced with those who rejoiced. He was hungry, he was weary, he was forsaken, betrayed, whipped, mocked and crucified but underneath it all, there was a foundation of joy.

Jesus pours his capacity for joy into us

The Lord desires for us to have his rock-solid joy. Jesus told his disciples in John 15:11, "I have told you these things so that you will be filled with my joy. Yes, your joy will overflow!" Jesus spoke these words because he knew that his disciples would be despondent and grief-stricken at his departure to heaven. He told them they would be comforted by the Holy Spirit.

The followers of Jesus experienced the joy he spoke about. After seeing Jesus' resurrection, his ascension, and after being filled with the Holy Spirit, neither beatings nor imprisonment could take away their joy. They sang and rejoiced even while in prison (Acts 16).

Jesus didn't present a fake smile to the world. He was authentic. In spite of all he went through, he had a deep and abiding joy. Hebrews 12:2, tells us why. "Because of the joy awaiting him, he endured the cross, disregarding its shame. Now he is seated in the place of honor beside God's throne." He kept his eye on his mission. It was for the joy of redeeming lost people like you and like me. He had his eyes on us and paid the ultimate price to ransom us back.

We too must keep God's promises in view even in the midst of our situation. We hold unto his promises because we know that God is on our side and that he loves us.

Joy brings strength into circumstances

In the Old Testament God told the children to celebrate time and time again. Nehemiah said, "Go and celebrate with a feast of rich foods and sweet drinks, and share gifts of food with people who have nothing prepared. This is a sacred day before our Lord. Don't be dejected and sad, for the joy of the Lord is your strength!" (Nehemiah 8:10).

Joy brings strength into circumstances! So it is safe to say that the absence of joy creates weakness. Complaining sucks strength out of you and causes unfavorable circumstances to seem even more dismal. On one occasion when the Israelites started to complain about their discontent in the wilderness, God destroyed some of them:

"Soon the people began to complain about their hardship, and the Lord heard everything they said. Then the Lord's anger blazed against them, and he sent a fire to rage among them, and he destroyed some of the people in the outskirts of the camp" (Numbers 11:1). The reason God hates complaining is because he knows it hurts you and takes you out of a position of strength. Joy is a spiritual strength that sustains you in any circumstance.

Joy opens doors for you

Although imprisoned unjustly, Paul and Silas chose to pray and sing instead of complain and grumble about their circumstances (Acts 16). They could have been saying, "We've been doing God's work all along. Why does he allow us to get treated like this?" But they didn't. They found joy as they sang hymns to God. When you have an attitude of joy at your very core it opens doors for you and allows miracles to happen in your life.

In Paul and Silas' experience, there was an earthquake and the whole prison was shaken to its foundation. The doors flew open and all the chains of every prisoner fell off. The jailer awoke to see the prison doors wide open, and he assumed the prisoners had escaped. He drew a sword to kill himself but Paul assured him that all the prisoners were still there. The jailer fell down, trembling before Paul and Silas and asked, "Sirs, what must I do to be saved?" Paul had the opportunity to lead the jailor's family to Christ and baptize them. Some historians believe that this jailer went on to become the leader of the church of Philippi.

I'm not a joyful person, how do I change?

First of all, you must choose to pursue joy now! It's a choice. Psalm 118:24 says, "This is the day the Lord has made. We will rejoice and be glad in it." That scripture sounds like we must *choose* and subsequently we *will* rejoice and be joyful. Every day when you get up in the morning, choose to say, "This is the day that the Lord has made. I will rejoice and be glad." Then when all those situations bombard you during the day, you will remember the choice you made early in the morning. If you wait until conditions are perfect you will not know the meaning of joy.

There are many situations in daily life that can try to steal your joy. I (Sam) was traveling with someone when another driver cut in front of us almost causing us to have an accident. I slammed on the brakes and my passenger exclaimed (to the other driver), "You idiot!"

I said, "How do you know that person's an idiot?"

"Well, he acts like an idiot," said my passenger.

I noticed that the other driver was an elderly gentleman who didn't look like an idiot at all. He was merely an elderly gentleman who had made an error in judging the speed of the oncoming traffic. He wasn't doing it on purpose. He wasn't an idiot; he had made a mistake. You must choose not to let the little things steal your joy. Choose today to rejoice and be glad in the Lord.

The second thing you need to do is to be intentional about associating with people who are joy carriers. I think we all know a few people in our lives who are joy carriers. You just love to be with them because they add joy to life—it's like they breathe life into you. Find some joy carrier relationships and become a joy carrier yourself.

Find some joy carrier relationships and become a joy carrier yourself.

Regardless of what we are going through, our God promises to give us "beauty for ashes, a joyous blessing instead of mourning, festive praise instead of despair..." (Isaiah 61:3). He also promises to turn our "mourning into joy" (Jeremiah 31:13). We can trust him!

Consider it pure joy when you face hard times

You may say, "Man, I'm having some hard times! Why me?" It is never easy when God allows us to go through hard times. It can make us feel like giving up when God doesn't make sense to us. What God really wants us to do is keep trusting him. This is why James 1:2-5 tells us, "Dear brothers and sisters, when troubles come your way, consider it an opportunity for great joy. For you know that when your faith is tested, your endurance has a chance to grow. So let it grow, for when your endurance is fully developed, you will be perfect and complete, needing nothing. If you need wisdom, ask our generous God, and he will give it to you. He will not rebuke you for asking."

When we understand that the trials of life can be used by the Lord to work his character in our lives, it really changes our perspective. We can rejoice, because the Lord is using it for our good! And he promises to give us wisdom right in the middle of the trials if we just ask him. He can be trusted, in spite of the pain.

When I (Larry) was a young man I drove an old beat up Volkswagen bug that seemed to be falling apart. When I drove on certain back roads in our county the steering wheel wobbled so much that I could hardly control the car. It was frustrating trying to drive that old jalopy, and I would find myself constantly losing my joy whenever this happened.

One day I decided to take this scripture literally and I began to personalize it to myself while driving. I told myself; "I consider driving this rattletrap an opportunity for great joy…because I know that my faith is tested, and endurance has a chance to grow. So let it grow, for when my endurance is fully developed, I will be perfect and complete, needing nothing." It was amazing. My whole attitude changed. Try it sometime, it really works!

I remember taking a course in high school to learn how to make certain metal tools. In order for the tools to be hardened, we were taught to take a hot molten piece of metal and dip it in and out of water in order to temper it. This process gave the tool the proper strength to be useful. Our Lord allows us to go through tough times in order to make us useful in his service. An attitude of pride will not hold up under pressure. When we go through some fiery trials in life and choose to walk in joy, we learn to trust in the Lord and in his word. His character is built into our lives. Without his character built into our lives, we will break under pressure when the Lord really begins to use us.

Persevering in our trials

Yes, the Lord will use us, even when we are going through hard times! For example, did you ever have a brother or sister "sandpaper" in your life—someone who rubbed you the wrong way? Maybe the Lord allowed this person in your life for a reason. Perhaps he wanted to see if you would respond in a Christ-like way. So you reached out to the Lord for his strength to love this person unconditionally. It was not easy, and life was unpleasant for a while, but you came through this experience with a new love and awareness of God's grace and mercy. Today you have a great relationship with this former

The trials of life can be used by the Lord to work his character in our lives.

"sister sandpaper." Why? Because choosing to release the joy of the Lord in your life and persevering really made you strong.

Invite joy into your life by staging celebrations. Find reasons to celebrate life as you go through your day. Jump for joy—as often as possible. Life is not meant to be endured; it is to be enjoyed. You are a child of God, and in his presence is "fullness of joy" (Psalm 16:11 NAS). Let's choose to operate in the joy Jesus gives today!

[1] Ron Hembree, *Fruit of the Spirit,* (Grand Rapid, MI, Baker Book House, 1969) pp. 31-32.

Fruit for Thought

1. How often did you laugh this week? How did it change your spiritual climate?

2. Are you able to choose joy in times of frustration or difficulty? How have you done it?

3. Describe a time joy brought strength to your circumstances.

Growing the Fruit of the Spirit

Chapter Five

Peace

"First keep the peace within yourself, then
you can also bring peace to others."
Thomas A Kempis

Not too long ago, the Worship Center, where I (Sam) serve as senior pastor, held a memorial service for Patsy Taylor. Pasty, her husband Andrew and their son Luke served as missionaries to India and the South Pacific for many years. Her thirteen-year-old son Luke stood up front at the service, his eyes brimming with tears, but with a smile on his face, and thanked God for the 13 years that he had with his mom. Where did he find such a peace in the midst of the death of a beloved mother? He had discovered God's peace, a virtue that was produced by the action of the Holy Spirit within him, that strengthened him spiritually.

Even at this young age, he was learning that Jesus is the peace and calm in the storms of life. In the Bible, after calming a storm that threatened to overturn the terrified disciples' boat, Jesus asked them why they were so afraid. Why didn't they trust him? Even though they had seen many miracles, they still didn't understand that they were always in his care (Mark 4:35-40).

The Bible says that the "*peace* of God, that is beyond all understanding, guards our hearts and minds" (Philippians 4:7). Another scripture says, "God, the source of hope, will fill you completely with joy and *peace* because you trust in him" (Romans 15:13). This is the peace Jesus gives. It is a state of being that causes us to trust him no matter what, because we realize we are in his care.

Peace is *freedom from disturbance or agitation.* A branch does not bear fruit by struggling, but by abiding in the vine. When you walk through a vineyard, do you detect tension and struggle among the branches as they bear fruit? No! Instead there is a calm and confident resting— an abiding—as branches draw their life from the vine in order to bear fruit.

How peace can be stolen

When we are at peace we are free of disquieting or oppressive thoughts or emotions. Nobody wishes for anxiety, panic attacks or worry. But we all have times our peace is tested. My peace was tested at the London airport just last week. I (Larry) was returning home from a trip to Africa via London. My plan was to arrive home briefly in Pennsylvania on Monday night and leave early the next day for Dallas. It was going to be a time crunch and everything had to go smoothly for it to happen. At the London airport, they informed me that my flight only allowed one carry on bag. I had two. I was directed to go through a long outside line with only 50 minutes to catch my connecting flight. By the grace of God I remained calm and made it within two minutes of my flight leaving.

The devil knows that one of the most treasured possessions you have is your peace of mind and peace of heart. As a thief, he's always looking for ways to steal your peace. **When peace operates in our lives, it releases the power of God to act.** Every moment he seeks entry into your life through strife, worry, doubt and fear—all in an attempt to rob your peace. When you lack peace you ultimately end up powerless. If you're filled with unrest, anxiety, and anguish of mind, you feel powerless to pursue your God-given purpose and dream in life.

When you are zeroed in on the anxiety and strife in life, it takes all the strength out of you because you are thinking about the worst thing that could happen.

It's hard to move ahead if you don't have peace. Without God's peace, that's what life is like—it's a cycle of worry, strife, doubt and fear, which leads to negative thoughts and actions that keep us powerless.

But there's good news. Life in the Spirit begins with peace. I'll never forget the day in February 1972 when I (Sam) gave my life to Christ. My life was a mess. I was filled with anxiety, misery, fear, and doubt. But all of that lifted, and peace came into my heart to stay. I no longer had to grasp for peace after that day. Christians have peace planted in their beings. Never again do they have to grasp for it because it is already in them. When peace operates in our lives, it releases the power of God to act.

Jesus came to give us peace

Peace is both a gift and a fruit. What do you do when somebody wants to give you a gift? You receive it. You don't pay for it. You receive it. It would be rather strange if at Christmastime you give your son or daughter a Christmas gift and they pull out their wallet and say, "How much is it? How much do I owe you?" That would be an insult to you.

Jesus left this earth with a promise of peace to believers, "I am leaving you with a gift—peace of mind and heart. And the peace I give is a gift the world cannot give. So don't be troubled or afraid" (John 14:27). Peace is a gift from Jesus, the Prince of Peace. The world's peace is momentary but God's peace is eternal. God's peace is independent of outward circumstances.

Think about it—because peace is planted in your heart, no matter what comes into your life, you can have peace. Jesus said in John 16:33 (AMP), "I've told you these things, so that in Me you may have perfect peace and confidence. In the world you may have trials and tribulations and distress and frustration. Be of good cheer, take courage, be confident, certain, undaunted for I have overcome the world. I have deprived it of power to harm you and I have conquered it for you."

The gospel is a gospel of peace. Romans 5:1 says, "Therefore since we are justified, (acquitted, declared righteous, given a right standing with God) through faith [let us grasp the fact that we have the peace of reconciliation to hold and to enjoy] peace with God through our Lord Jesus Christ (the Messiah, the anointed one)." You can look for peace everywhere but you cannot get lasting peace except by coming to Christ. Jesus came to make peace between God and man. The gift of peace will change the way you live.

Peace in our mind and heart allows us to hear God more clearly

Colossians 3:15 (AMP) tells us, "And let the peace (soul harmony which comes) from Christ rule (act as umpire continually) in your hearts [deciding and settling with finality all questions that arise in your minds, in that peaceful state] to which as [members of Christ's] one body you were also called [to live]. And be thankful (appreciative), [giving praise to God always]."

I (Sam) don't normally watch baseball, but when the World Series is on, I watch this championship series culminating the major league baseball season. The guy behind the plate is the umpire and makes all the decisions. It doesn't matter if the manager tries to dispute a call. I've seen a manager angrily spitting at an umpire and kicking dust in his face; nevertheless, the decision the umpire makes is final.

Scripture says that peace in your heart should be your final decision-maker (your umpire). Peace is that velvety, green-light feeling you have on the inside. The other side is that scratchy, red-light kind of feeling, and whenever we have that, we shouldn't move ahead.

I'm sure all of us can point to times when we had a lack of peace and we moved ahead anyway, and it affected our lives in a negative way. Learn to be led by the peace you have within. Lay your decisions on the scales of peace. If you don't have peace about it, don't move ahead. Peace is an "inner knowing" that our actions are approved by God.

Philippians 4:6-7 says, "Don't worry about anything; instead, pray about everything. Tell God what you need, and thank him for all he has done. Then you will experience God's peace, which exceeds anything we can understand. His peace will guard your hearts and minds as you live in Christ Jesus." Tell God your needs and don't forget to thank him for his answers.

If you do this you will experience God's peace. Why do we make it so complicated? That sounds really simple, which is far more wonderful than the human mind can understand. His peace will keep our thoughts and our hearts quiet and at rest as we trust in Christ Jesus.

The moment you begin to worry, pray instead. 1 Peter 5:7 says, "Give all your worries and cares to God, for he cares about you. He's always thinking about you." Some time ago, my (Sam's) brother-in-law Glenn had a near fatal motorcycle accident. The first couple of days in the hospital they were not sure if he would make it. To further compound his many problems, the doctor told my sister Becky that Glenn had ARDS disease. ARDS disease is a disease that can attack the lungs when they are collapsed. The lung needs to be kept moving and breathing and soft, but if it does not respond to treatment the lung hardens and the person dies. When the doctors presented that information to Becky, it was just more bad news. Glenn was teetering between life and death, and now he had ARDS disease.

Don't wait until worry has grabbed a hold of you. Pray right away because prayer transfers the problem from you to Jesus.

I loved how Becky reacted. Like a fruit that is squeezed, we got to know what was on the inside of Becky. Her foundation with God was strong, and she refused to worry. Upon the doctor's bad news, she came to us and said, "Now this is what the doctors said, but we want to tell you what we're believing. Here is what we want you to pray and believe with us for," and she listed the prayer requests. Day after day, she or her daughter Shawna would say, "This is Glenn's condition, but this is what we're believing for today." (It is now months later and Glenn is doing just great. He is back to work and has exceeded the doctors' expectations. His healing has been a great testimony of God's power and grace.)

Don't worry about anything. Pray about everything. Don't wait until worry has grabbed a hold of you. Pray right away because prayer transfers the problem from you to Jesus.

Peace brings rest and confidence and hope in God

The story of Daniel being thrown into the lions' den is an account of placing one's complete trust and confidence in God. Daniel was a principled man who gained the favor of King Darius who gave him sole administrative authority over his kingdom. This made others jealous, and they sought a way to discredit Daniel. They convinced Darius to make it mandatory for all his subjects to worship him for the next 30 days and anyone caught worshiping anyone else would be thrown into a den of hungry lions.

Daniel remained true to his God and continued his practice of praying three times a day. Of course, the others reported Daniel's disobedience to the King. The king was distressed because he liked Daniel, but he couldn't save him from the decree he had signed. So Daniel was thrown into the den. The king spent a restless, stressful night, but Daniel was at peace. How could he be at peace during one of the toughest nights of his life? He was falsely accused and thrown to the lions. It can't get much worse than that! But Daniel's trust and hope was in God. He probably used one of the lions for his pillow!

As a pastor, I (Sam) am sometimes in a room when a believer leaves this earth to be with Jesus. When my mom was passing on, my siblings and I were by her bed. During the last hours before she left she said, "I see a spiral staircase, and it's on the other side of a river. There's someone at the bottom of the staircase dressed in white beckoning for me to come."

We said, "Well mom, go ahead!" She talked to us about five more minutes before she left. I don't know if I've ever experienced such a tangible peace. We knew she was stepping into a new, wonderful and amazing place. Her confidence was in God.

Living life with purpose brings peace

Having a sense of direction and purpose gives us peace through the storms because we know where we are headed. Being in a storm without a destination—how scary is that? The peace of the world offers purpose focused on self-fulfillment. God's peace comes from a purpose focused on God and others.

You may say, "I'm just a grocery store checker, my job has no meaning. I just go to work every day and endure it. It doesn't have any purpose." Why not put some meaning and purpose into it? Instead of haphazardly throwing that loaf of bread into the bag, pray for the person. Sow seeds of encouragement into a person's life.

There's a story of a grocery store checker who did just that. He started placing a little piece of paper that had a message of hope on it in every bag. In a little while the grocery store manager didn't know what to do because everybody wanted that checker. Nobody wanted to go to any other check-out line, because everybody wants hope and encouragement.

If you approach your jobs that way—by being faithful with what God has given you now, God will open doors of opportunity you never thought of before and you will experience great peace from him!

We can be peacemakers

Matthew 5:9 says, "God blesses those who work for peace, for they will be called the children of God." We can be the ones that bring peace into a situation. I (Sam) grew up in a home with twelve siblings. Believe me, we got in some fights! There were times when Mom just turned her head away and said, "Well, just kill each other if you want to. I'll pick up the pieces later."

Sometimes a wrestling match would start out as fun and get ugly because we'd get mad and refuse to give up. Often, my brother Crit, (his real name is Christian) would come and disentangle two wrestling brothers and help them resolve their differences. We called him our peacemaker. I'm glad there was one peacemaker in our family!

Growing the Fruit of the Spirit

Living in the peace of God—what an amazing way to live in the midst of a world of turmoil. I (Sam) was driving in my car one day and I felt these words come up out of my spirit. So, as soon as I got home I wrote them down.

"The fruit of the Spirit are forces of the Spirit. It's not like putting your car in neutral and staying at the same place. The fruit of the Spirit are forces that will penetrate through the heart of a person and open the door for that person for Christ. So, when we're talking about putting on the character of Christ we're talking about power. We're talking about projection. We're not just talking about some meek little dreamy feeling—"I'm so peaceful…." No, we're talking about people who are clothed with the character of Christ. And we're going to make a difference in our world for Jesus!"

Let's put our car in "drive" and intentionally work for peace in our own lives as well as bringing peace to others.

Fruit for Thought

1. How has peace in your heart enabled you to hear from God more clearly?

2. To what degree are your heart and mind at peace in God? How can your peace be stolen?

3. How have you been a peace-maker?

Chapter Six

Patience

"Patience is the ability to count down
before you blast off."

Author Unknown

One time when I told somebody I was preaching on patience, he started laughing. I (Sam) said, "Why are you laughing?" And he laughed some more. I continued, "Are you saying I have a reputation for having a lack of patience?" At that, he laughed uncontrollably! I will admit that patience is probably the fruit of the Spirit that needs the most work in my life.

We did a quick online survey of people within our congregation, asking them which character traits of the fruit of the Spirit that they felt they needed the most help with. The number one response was "patience." Self-control came in a close second.

If I want my life to display the character of Jesus and become more like him, I must conduct myself in a manner that reflects that character, including the fruit of patience. Scriptures say we should be like a sweet perfume to those around us.

People should smell something different about us: "But thank God! He has made us his captives and continues to lead us along in Christ's triumphal procession. Now he uses us to spread the knowledge of Christ everywhere, like a sweet perfume" (2 Corinthians 2:14). We are the aroma of Christ to those we come into contact with.

Growing in God's character is a life long journey.

Another place in scripture, Peter and John healed a lame man and were called before the religious leaders who did not approve. They were, however, impressed by the fact that they had been with Jesus. "The members of the council were amazed when they saw the boldness of Peter and John, for they could see that they were ordinary men with no special training in the Scriptures. They also recognized them as men who had been with Jesus" (Acts 4:13).

Do your neighbors and co-workers know by the way you live, by the way you talk and act that you have been with Jesus? Growing in God's character is a life long journey. No matter how many years we live here on this earth it will be a growing process all the way to the end.

What is patience?

One dictionary tells us that patience is "that quality of self-restraint in the face of provocation which does not

Growing the Fruit of the Spirit

hastily retaliate." It's the opposite of anger, and is associated with mercy. The Webster's 1828 dictionary gives this definition: "The quality of waiting long for justice or expected good without discontent; a calm temper which bears evil without murmuring or discontent. Perhaps you've been mistreated or offended and it seems as if you are waiting a long time for justice to be served. If you are content during your wait, and refuse to complain, you are learning how to be patient.

Here's another definition of patience: "The quality that does not surrender to circumstances or succumb under trial." It is the opposite of despondency, and is associated with hope. Patience is bearing pain and trials calmly or without complaint. It is remaining steadfast, despite opposition, difficulty or adversity. It's an amazing word— an amazing force. It's so powerful, and that's why the enemy fights it so hard, because the opposite of patience is irritation, or anger, or prematurely acting on something. The end result of irritation and anger gets us in trouble and often hurts people.

Patience is not letting go of your dream from God

Habakkuk, a prophet from the Old Testament, said, "I will climb up to my watchtower and stand at my guard post. There I will wait to see what the Lord says and how he will answer my complaint. Then the Lord said to me, 'Write my answer plainly on tablets…This vision is for a future time. It describes the end, and it will be fulfilled. If it seems slow in coming, wait patiently, for it will surely take place. It will not be delayed'" (Habakkuk 2:1-3).

Whenever God speaks concerning his unfolding plan, believers know they have no choice but to wait on him. We are compelled to wait patiently on the Lord, all the while being fully convinced of his timing faithfulness. My (Sam's) administrative assistant told me her story of praying for a husband. As she was believing and praying for a husband, she felt like the Holy Spirit showed her who it would be. She didn't tell anybody.

She had the right idea, because that information should be kept private between you and God. I know of one person that believed the Holy Spirit told him a certain woman was going to be his bride and when he told her, she said, "Well that's strange, because I'm already married!"

Back to my administrative assistant. She stayed quiet about what God had revealed to her. Three years went by. Three long years. I asked her, "Cammi what did you do for three years?"

She said, "I took that time to go deeper with God." There it is! Simple and profound: if you are waiting for something, go deeper with God!

Three years went by and the man God revealed to her finally asked for Cammi's hand in marriage. She was ecstatic. Her dream came to pass. This is just an example of patiently waiting after you receive a vision from the Lord.

I asked Cammi, "Did you ever feel like letting go of your vision?"

She said, "Are you kidding? I was tempted to let go so many times. But every time I was tempted it seemed like God would give added grace to me, just to keep standing."

If you have a dream or vision in your heart that you feel God has given you, hold onto it. God wants to give you the desires of your heart. "Take delight in the Lord, and he will give you your heart's desires. Commit everything you do to the Lord. Trust him, and he will help you" (Psalm 37:4-5). You must remain pliable and patiently surrendered to God and he promises to give you your heart's desires.

> **Patience means making a daily decision to trust and obey God, even when things aren't going the way you planned.**

I (Sam) met a man in India years ago who was my interpreter. He had a vision to start a church of his own in another town, so he rented a room and advertised it. Sunday came and no one showed up. "What did you do?" I asked.

"I preached to the walls and the chairs," he said. "I conducted the whole service without anyone being there." The next Sunday came, and no one was there except for the preacher, who again preached to the walls and the chairs. It was three months before anyone came. Today, he has a thriving church between 300 to 400 people. The power of patience! Patience means making a daily decision to trust and obey God, even when things aren't going the way you planned.

Patience in our interaction with people

You could call this "daily day-to-day patience." This is where the rubber meets the road! Colossians 3:12-13 says, "...clothe yourselves with tenderhearted mercy, kindness, humility, gentleness, and patience. Make allowance for each other's faults, and forgive anyone who offends you. Remember, the Lord forgave you, so you must forgive others."

God is patient with you. He is patient with you when you get angry in traffic or irritated in the grocery store while waiting in a long line. You know what I mean. You can feel the road rage boiling up when that guy cuts in front of you or blows his horn behind you. How many times have you gone to the grocery store and wanted to go through the express check out that indicates you should have under 6 items and the person in front of you has about 25 items in his cart? You start to feel irritated and angry.

The Lord knows we both need patience, and he tests us often! And frequently in places like grocery stores. I (Larry) have waited in line "forever" due to picking the "wrong" checkout line so many times I have stopped counting. I (Sam) was in the grocery store once and looking for an express check-out lane because I had just two items: a half a gallon of milk and a box of laundry soap.

There was no express lane, so I reluctantly got in line behind people with huge cartloads of groceries to check out. When I finally was the next in line to pay, the person in front of me poured out all her loose change on the conveyer belt, and meticulously started counting. She literally counted out one hundred and fifty pennies to finish paying her bill! Surprise, surprise, I was irritated!

On the way home from the grocery store, I felt the Holy Spirit getting my attention. "What if that was the only money she had? What if her children were sick and she was counting out her last pennies to buy them some food? Why didn't you pray for her, instead of getting annoyed?"

When your faith is tested, it grows *patience*, producing that powerful force in the Spirit that holds you steady.

Unless we practice patience we will often misunderstand or misjudge people. If we really knew what was going on in others' lives we would be more patient with them.

A story is told by the famed evangelist, Sam Jones. The train was filled with tired persons, most of whom spent the day traveling through the hot plains. At last evening came and all tried to settle down to a sound sleep. However, at one end of the car a man was holding a tiny baby and as night came on the baby became restless and cried more and more.

Unable to take it any longer, a big, brawny man spoke for the rest of the group. "Why don't you take that baby to its mother?" There was a moment's pause and then came the reply. "I'm sorry. I'm doing my best. The baby's mother is in her casket in the baggage car ahead."

Again there was an awful silence for a moment. Then the big man who asked the cruel question was out of his seat and moved toward the man with the motherless child. He apologized for his impatience and unkind remark. He took the tiny baby in his own arms and told the tired father to get some sleep. In loving patience he cared for the little child all through the night.[1]

Patience is a powerful character builder

Remember what James said, "Dear brothers and sisters, when troubles come your way, consider it an opportunity for great joy. For you know that when your faith is tested, your endurance has a chance to grow. So let it grow, for when your endurance is fully developed, you will be perfect and complete, needing nothing" (James 1:1-4).

When your faith is tested, it grows *patience*, producing that powerful force in the Spirit that holds you steady. Just because something you are waiting for hasn't happened yet doesn't mean God has changed his mind. While you are waiting, God is working in the unseen realm. Impatience is a sign of immaturity. Satan tries to keep you from developing patience because if he can get you irritated and angry, it will be harder to hear from God.

Our culture knows very little about waiting because we have developed so many instant things. If we don't receive our hamburger in 90 seconds as expected, we want to storm into the fast food establishment and talk to the manager. We have instant credit where we can buy now and pay later. But if we choose to allow patience to grow in us, we will reach the place where the enemy can no longer control us. The Lord wants us to relax and enjoy the wait in his "waiting room" by allowing the fruit of his patience to flow through us and enter into his joy.

[1]   John M. Drescher, *Spirit Fruit*, (Scottdale, PA: Herald Press, 1974), p.186

Fruit for Thought

1. How do you react when people aren't moving as quickly as you would like? How do you react when God is not moving as quickly as you want?

2. How do you respond when you don't get your way or you're frustrated?

3. Describe how patience was "not letting go of your dream from God."

Chapter Seven

Kindness

"I expect to pass through life but once. If
therefore, there be any kindness I can show,
or any good thing I can do to any fellow-
being, let me do it now, and not defer or
neglect it, as I shall not pass this way again."
William Penn

There is the story of the mother who sought to repri-
mand her quarrelling children. She encouraged them to
be "kind" to one another. When her daughter inquired what
"kind" meant, the mother carefully explained the term.
The child then asked: "Mom, do we know anyone like
that?"

Kindness is one of fruit of godly Christian character
you grow which helps you get fit for life! It does not just
happen. Like the other fruit of the Spirit, kindness is within
each Christian in seed form, but it must be grown through
the action of the Holy Spirit within you, otherwise it will
not be evident.

Colossians 3:12,14 says it another way. It mentions that you must "clothe" yourself with kindness. "Since God chose you to be the holy people he loves, you must clothe yourselves with tenderhearted mercy, kindness, humility, gentleness, and patience...

Kindness is within each Christian in seed form, but it must be grown through the action of the Holy Spirit within.

Above all, clothe yourselves with love, which binds us all together in perfect harmony." God hand-picked a wardrobe of love for you, and kindness is one of its garments!

When you become a believer in Christ and are born again, you are made holy, and all the character traits of God come into your recreated human spirit. You don't have to try to get them, they're already there. You do, however, need to develop them. They are within you in seed form and will remain in seed form unless you do something about it. So, that is the action part for you. Your clothes don't automatically jump on you in the morning. You have to put them on piece by piece. And that's the way it is with the character of God, you have to put on every piece of the wardrobe that he picked out for you.

It is said that in the ancient world the early Christians were sometimes called the "Kind Ones" rather than "Christians." This is due in part to the fact that there is just one letter of difference in the word for Christ (*christos*) and the word for kindness (*chrestotes*). People were confused about the name.

When you think about kindness or a kind person what comes to your mind? I (Larry) have to say that unequivocally my wife is one of kindest people in the world. LaVerne models kindness for me. We all know someone in our lives who has a kind disposition that delights in contributing to the happiness of others without expecting to receive anything in return. These people love to give selflessly as they go about cheering up others. They generally love to make people smile or be happier.

In today's world, kindness can be a scarce commodity. We are stressed out, frazzled and in a hurry to go places. This lowers our tolerance for others' mistakes, and we often behave impatiently rather than kindly. To be kind takes deliberate intention and effort to practice in today's fast-paced world. Not too many years ago, a non-profit organization called "The Random Acts of Kindness Foundation" started to inspire people to practice kindness and to "pass it on" to others. We really can't have too much kindness in the world. By choosing to show kindness to those around us each day, we are contributing to the happiness of others.

Kindness reaches out

Kindness cannot exist in a vacuum. Kindness reaches out. It's thinking of others first. Kindness is the opposite of self-centeredness. I like how the apostle Paul put it in Philippians, chapter 2, verse 3-4. "Don't be selfish; don't try to impress others. Be humble, thinking of others as better than yourselves. Don't look out only for your own interests, but take an interest in others, too." Kindness is an unselfish mindset that takes a genuine interest in other people. Kindness is thinking of others and extending our love to them for no other reason except that we care.

An 85-year-old man used to eat breakfast in a Kroger supermarket every morning. He was bossy, very particular, and even remarked that the female employees could stand to lose weight.

A few weeks after the old man died of cancer, several of the shocked clerks received checks for $10,000 from his estate. Why? Even when the old man had been cranky and insulting, the staff waiting on him had treated him pleasantly and tried to cheer him up with a little tender care! They even went beyond the call of duty by taking turns to visit him in the hospital! Clearly, none of them expected anything in return.

There's a word for what the Kroger staff extended to him—kindness. But if you are a follower of Jesus, then kindness has to be what you dish out on a regular basis.[1]

You may not always reap immediate, tangible benefits of kindness, but treating people with kindness keeps your approach to life on the right track. Being kind gets you out of the *what will they do for me* world and gets your heart in tune with *what can I do for them?*

Take the time to smile and greet people. Something as simple as your tone of voice can open the heart of a person. There are many daily ways to show kindness if you program yourself to look out for the interests of others. Jesus said that when we display outward works of love and kindness to those who have a need or are suffering, we are doing it for him (Matthew 25:40).

Kindness is appreciating differences

It would be boring if we were all the same. When we appreciate the difference in people we discover that most people have similar fears and hopes. Kindness is taking the time to understand another person's viewpoint. A kind person will take the time to understand something and not make a judgment just because someone does something differently than you.

Sherlyn and I (Sam) often go out for breakfast on Monday mornings on my day off. I like a leisurely breakfast where I can take my time and relax. We were having such a breakfast, or at least I thought, until I realized we had a waitress who was very much in a rush. Everything she did seemed abrupt and hurried. I didn't like being rushed, and she was starting to annoy me.

To make matters worse, she handed me my glass by the part my lips touch. How unsanitary! So, I started grumbling to Sherlyn. She cut me short, "Sam, get a life," she said, "How does this little annoyance in your life compare to eternity? You don't know what she's going through. Let's be kind." She was right, of course!

By offering daily expressions of kindness, you can change someone's outlook for the day. The way you interact with people and acknowledge them can make a difference in their lives. We can release the fruit of kindness by finding opportunities to be considerate; like holding the door for somebody or letting someone into traffic in front of you or paying for someone's meal.

One time at a restaurant I (Sam) told my waitress that I wanted the check for the people at the next table. I didn't know who they were. Later, I discovered they knew me because they come to the church I pastor! Another time, I paid for the carload behind me at a drive through restaurant. I didn't stay around to see their reaction, but I'm sure it was a pleasant surprise for them.

Kindness is doing good when you feel you have the right to retaliate

We have been talking about the kindnesses we should express in daily life as we respond to others by being kind instead of petty. Now, we want to take you into a deeper level of kindness that goes deeper in our spirit. It's a whole new level of kindness. When we were at our worst: disobedient and enslaved to sin, God demonstrated his kindness and love to us by saving us and washing away our sins. This is love in return for hostility at its very best.

Once we, too, were foolish and disobedient. We were misled and became slaves to many lusts and pleasures. Our lives were full of evil and envy, and we hated each other. But—when God our Savior revealed his kindness and love, he saved us, not because of the righteous things we had done, but because of his mercy. He washed away our sins, giving us a new birth and new life through the Holy Spirit (Titus 3:3-5).

This kind of love expressed in the face of antagonism is the sort of kindness God wants us to express to our fellow man as well, according to Luke 6:27-31.

Find opportunities to be considerate.

But to you who are willing to listen, I say, love your enemies! Do good to those who hate you. Bless those who curse you. Pray for those who hurt you. If someone slaps you on one cheek, offer the other cheek also. If someone demands your coat, offer your shirt also. Give to anyone who asks; and when things are taken away from you, don't try to get them back. Do to others as you would want them to do to you.

Jesus knew it is not easy to do what he is suggesting—turning the other cheek when we feel we have the right to retaliate—but if we are "willing to listen" he will build his character in us. Too often we want to respond to being wronged by a desire to retaliate, like this truck driver:

"A weary truck driver pulled his rig into an all-night truck stop. He was tired and hungry. The waitress had just served him when three tough looking, leather jacketed motorcyclists decided to give him a hard time. One grabbed the hamburger off his plate, another took a handful of his french fries, and the third picked up his coffee and began to drink it.

"How did this trucker respond? Well, this trucker did not respond as one might expect. Instead, he calmly rose, picked up his check, walked to the front of the room, put the check and his money on the cash register, and went out the door. The waitress followed him to put the money in the till and stood watching out the door as the big truck drove away into the night.

"When she returned, one of the cyclists said to her, 'Well, he's not much of a man, is he?'

Love expressed in the face of antagonism is the sort of kindness God wants us to express.

"She replied, 'I don't know about that, but he sure isn't much of a truck driver. He just ran over three motorcycles on his way out of the parking lot.'"[2]

We chuckle at this story because we know there have been times we have wanted to do what this trucker did and retaliate. However, if we are willing to listen to Jesus, and allow him to build his character in us, we will choose kindness even when we feel we have the right to retaliate.

Remember God's kindness toward you

The greatest act of kindness was when God sent his son to the earth to redeem mankind. The kindness of God was extended to everyone. This unfailing kindness expresses how to show kindness to others. Kindness is love directed toward others for their sake and not just our own. Kindness is not a virtue that can be developed in isola-

Growing the Fruit of the Spirit

tion. Kindness is all about the quality of our relationships with one another.

I have a pastor friend who calls me almost every week and he'll say, "Pastor Sam, I love you and there's nothing you can do about it!" I like that. I could reject that offer of love or receive it. Well, I receive it from him; he's a great guy.

And so it is with the kindness of God. We can reject it or we can receive it, by receiving his son Jesus Christ, and then walk in the fruit of kindness every day. All of us need his forgiveness; we need his love; we need his kindness to take root in our lives, and we need to find opportunities every day to give the fruit of kindness away.

[1] *Daily Strength* with Joel Stowell, www.rbc.org/bible-study/strength-for-the-journey/2008/04/21/daily-message.aspx, accessed May 2008.

[2] "Blind and Toothless" by J. David Hoke, www.horizonsnet.org/sermons/sm17.html, accessed May 2008.

Fruit for Thought

1. How do you encourage and affirm people? Are you inclined to do it consistently?

2. How does kindness reach out? For example, do you offer a helping hand even though you won't get the recognition?

3. Have you ever felt you had the right to retaliate but instead turned the other cheek? Describe this kind of kindness.

Growing the Fruit of the Spirit

Chapter Eight

Goodness

"Do all the good you can, in all the ways you
can, to all the souls you can, in every place you
can, at all the times you can, with all the zeal
you can, as long as ever you can."

John Wesley

Goodness is a fruit of the Spirit that's a bit difficult to
define because it is so general in nature. In fact, goodness
is probably easier to recognize than to define. Goodness
"signifies not merely goodness as a quality, rather it is
goodness in action, goodness expressing itself in deeds."[1]

We find an excellent biblical example of goodness in
the story of the Good Samaritan. Although others passed
by the beaten man along the road, maybe because they
considered him beyond help or they didn't want to get
their hands dirty, the Good Samaritan went beyond what
was expected of him. Out of the goodness of his heart, he
showed kindness and generosity. He was open-hearted and
open-handed—and that is probably a good definition of

goodness. Goodness is kindness and love shown to others as it is manifested in action. Goodness is love in action. Here is an inspiring account of a man brimming with goodness:

> George Washington Carver was a man who had this special goodness. Born a slave, Carver struggled against tremendous odds to achieve an education. Finally, after years of abuse he finished his master's degree and was asked to accept a position with Iowa University. It was a coveted job and no other Negro had ever had such a high place. At last he could relax and enjoy the comforts of his society. People at the university loved him and sat eagerly in his classes.
>
> Then a letter came from Booker T. Washington asking the young scientist to join him in a dream to educate Negroes of the South. Leaving his comfortable position, Carver traveled to the parched cotton lands of the South to live and work among his starving people. Years of sacrifice and insult followed, but slowly and surely this great soul saved his people from sure starvation and brought them a dignity that would raise them forever from the slave class.

When questioned about his brilliance, Carver always said the good Lord gave him everything. He refused to accept money for any of his discoveries, rather choosing to give them free to anyone who asked for them. Three presidents claimed him as a friend. Great industries vied for his service and even Thomas Edison offered him a beautiful new laboratory and a $100,000 a year salary. When Carver turned it down critics commented, "If you had all this money you could help your people." Carver simply replied, "If I had all that money I might forget my people." The epitaph on his tomb bears the sacred soul of this great man, "He could have added fame and fortune, but cared for neither, he found happiness and honor in being helpful to the world." This type of goodness always costs greatly.[2]

Goodness goes hand-in-hand with the love we have for our fellow man and the kindness we show to them by doing what is good. Goodness comes from a place in our hearts,

Goodness comes from a place in our hearts, but it always requires action.

but it always requires action. When we think of someone who has the fruit of goodness, we think of someone who makes an intentional effort to be charitable, compassionate, generous, and displays empathy for others. It comes from a focus on how we speak and act toward one another. It is important for us to ask ourselves how we would feel if we were treated the way we are treating others.

The source of goodness

To be sure, we cannot be good on our own steam. Goodness is a fruit of the Spirit and comes only by the power of the Spirit. Our natural tendency is to be selfish and sinful. One day, a man came to Jesus, expecting to find goodness in others and wanting to be good himself so he could be deserving of heaven. He asked, "Good Teacher, what must I do to inherit eternal life?"

"Why do you call me good?" Jesus asked. "Only God is truly good" (Mark 10:17-18). In his reply, Jesus was not denying his divinity, but was simply enlightening the man to the truth that goodness is not natural to the human heart and none of us can deserve eternal life.

But what prevents us from being consistently good? The answer is simply "sin." Without Christ, we are all predisposed to self-centeredness. It's a good thing that Romans 12:21 tells us that goodness overcomes evil.

In fact, Romans chapter 12 gives us some very interesting instructions. We are told to heap burning coals on our enemies head. What is that all about?

If your enemies are hungry, feed them. If they are thirsty, give them something to drink. In doing this, you will heap burning coals of shame on their heads. Don't let evil conquer you, but conquer evil by doing good (Romans 12:20-21).

How is heaping coals of fire on someone's head releasing the spiritual fruit of goodness? How is this overcoming evil with good?

When Paul the apostle was inspired by God to write this letter to the Romans, everyone was familiar with the hot days and cold nights in the desert. The shepherds needed to keep a fire burning all night to stay warm. When a shepherd's fire went out, he could become sick or even die in the desert. Coals for building fires were carried in a basket on the heads of the shepherds.

Only God's goodness is absolute. We merely have degrees of goodness as measured against this absolute standard.

So when a shepherd realized that the fire had gone out for another shepherd, even his enemy, he gave him a few of his hot coals to relight the fire. Although his enemy had wronged him, he was heaping coals of fire on his head or warming him, and by extension, blessing him to give him life and health. He was modeling the fruit of goodness, and thereby, overcoming evil with good.

Find ways to bless those who have sinned against you. Overcome evil with good. Release the fruit of goodness in your life.

Only God's goodness is absolute. We merely have degrees of goodness as measured against this absolute standard. God is the ultimate source of all goodness. God describes himself as "abundant in goodness" (Exodus 34:6 KJV). Psalm 119:68 describes the Lord as good: "You are good, and do only good; teach me your decrees." The very essence of God is that he is good. But let's take the measure of goodness that the Lord has given to us and give it freely to others.

What is goodness, and what does it require?

The Israelites asked God, "What do you want us to do to please you?" God essentially replies with this answer, "I've already *told* you!" He says in Micah 6:8, "...the Lord has told you what is good, and this is what he requires of you: to do what is right, to love mercy, and to walk humbly with your God."

The Lord was driving the point home that their failure was not necessarily because they neglected to give offerings or gifts to God, but because they had failed to be generous and merciful to one another. They lay awake at night thinking up ways to seize each other's property (Micah 2:2), ran after "ill-gotten treasures" (Micah 6:10) and used "dishonest scales" (Micah 6:11). Their business practices exploited other people (Micah 3:10), and their rich were violent and oppressive (Micah 6:12).

What God wanted from Micah's generation and from ours today is for his people to look squarely at the goodness he has shown and to respond by showing justice, mercy, and humility in the details of our lives. We can fulfill God's requirements to live "what is good" by acting toward God and others according to God's divine standard of righteousness. We must show a compassionate warm-heartedness and mercy toward others, and walk humbly in recognition of the absolute holiness and goodness of God.

Most of us know people who model the fruit of goodness. My wife LaVerne and I (Larry) were both brought up in homes where our parents modeled goodness. Even today, with my parents in their eighties and LaVerne's mother in her **Show a compassionate warm-heartedness and mercy toward others.** nineties (her father went to be with the Lord in 2007); they continue to model the fruit of goodness. They both continue to live in their homes and offer hospitality to those who stop in to see them. LaVerne's father was well known in his community as a loving generous farmer who would do anything for anyone. He modeled the fruit of goodness.

I have been so blessed by my parents over the years, because I grew up in a home where they refused to gossip and slander, but instead offered gifts of blessing to the unlovable and spoke well of others. My mother still opens up her dining room table and has guests in our home as a blessing to them. And they love helping the elderly who cannot give back to them in return. Their lives have modeled the fruit of goodness for me. I have been the recipient of the goodness of God through them.

Goodness means love in action. It's the sum total of

godliness in every area of thought and action. Goodness is living out love and showing kindness to others. And it is one of God's exercises to getting fit and healthy in your spiritual life.

[1] W. E. Vine, *Vine's Expository Dictionary of Old and New Testament Words*, (Old Tappan, NJ: Fleming H Revell Company, 1981).
[2] Ron Hembree, *Fruit of the Spirit,* (Grand Rapids, MI, Baker Book House, 1969) pp. 79-80

Fruit for Thought

1. How have you been generous and shown mercy to others? What quantity of your time and resources are you giving to God and others?

2. What does goodness require of you? Are you growing or dwindling in goodness?

3. Describe how you have shown goodness to someone who has sinned against you. How did you overcome evil with good?

Chapter Nine

Faithfulness

"We must do our business faithfully, without
trouble or disquiet, recalling our mind to God
mildly, and with tranquility, as often as we
find it wandering from him."
Brother Lawrence

A few years ago, LaVerne and I (Larry) and two of
our children visited Old Faithful, a cone geyser located in
Wyoming, in Yellowstone National Park, in the United
States. This geyser can shoot up to 8,400 gallons of boiling water to a height of 184 feet. Although impressive, it
is not the largest geyser in the Park, nor does it reach the
highest height, but it is by far the most popular. Why? It is
regular and dependable and thus its name, Old Faithful.
People flock to see it, because they can count on it to erupt
at regular intervals. And this brings us to God's seventh
exercise to spiritual fitness—faithfulness.

My (Larry) parents are in their eighties, but they still
run a business. They own a flower farm, raising chrysan-

themums. I'm amazed at their stamina and perseverance. As their son, I can trust them because my whole life I've watched them and I know their track record. I can count on them. They are faithful to their God and to their family, church and community. They live a life-style filled with faithfulness that backs up what they're saying. They are in it for the long haul.

Faithfulness is an essential attribute of God's character. It goes without saying that God is faithful. He can be depended on. You can count on him. We read in 2 Timothy 2:13; "If we are unfaithful, he remains faithful, for he cannot deny who he is." It would be a denial of God's very own nature for him to be anything other than perfectly faithful.

Other words for *faithfulness* are "reliability, trustworthiness, established, firm, permanent, content, supportive, steadfastness." When you think of a faithful person, what comes to your mind? You often think of someone who does what he promises, and you can count on him not to desert or betray you. You think of an individual who is faithful to his word. He is constant and not fickle.

God is looking for faithful people

God is looking for people willing to live a life of faithfulness. Faithfulness will spill out into every area of a believer's life. As Christians, God expects us to be of the 24 hour a day variety. Quite often, in today's world, people don't understand the reality of commitment—job-hopping, marriage hopping, church hopping—they all add up to looking after our own selfish needs rather than persevering when the going gets tough. Proverbs asks the question, "Most men will proclaim each his own goodness, but who can find a faithful man?" (Proverbs 20:6 NKJ).

The Bible says that Moses "served faithfully when he was entrusted with God's entire house" (Hebrews 3:2). Why did God consider him faithful? He faithfully taught the people and **Faithfulness will spill out into every area of a believer's life.**
discharged his duty in the household of God. With all the rebellion of the Israelites, he remained firm and unwavering and faithful.

Certainly, there had to be some days he didn't feel like pressing on, but he did. That's faithfulness for the long-haul. More than twenty-five years ago I (Larry) visited Koinonia Farm in Americus, Georgia. Here I learned the story of Clarence Jordan, a modern-day example of the faithfulness of God.

> Clarence Jordan was a man of unusual abilities and commitment. He had two Ph.D.s, one in agriculture and one in Greek and Hebrew. He was so gifted that he could have chosen to do anything he wanted. He chose to serve the poor.
>
> In the 1940s, he founded a farm in Americus, Georgia, and called it Koinonia Farm. It was a community for poor whites and poor blacks. As

you might guess, such an idea did not go over well in the Deep South of the '40s. Ironically, much of the resistance came from good church people who followed the laws of segregation as much as the other folk in town. The town people tried everything to stop Clarence. They tried boycotting him, and slashing workers' tires when they came to town. Over and over, for fourteen years, they tried to stop him.

Finally, in 1954, the Ku Klux Klan had enough of Clarence Jordan, so they decided to get rid of him once and for all. They came one night with guns and torches and set fire to every building on Koinonia Farm but Clarence's home, which they riddled with bullets. And they chased off all the families except one black family which refused to leave.

Clarence recognized the voices of many of the Klansmen, and, as you might guess, some of them were church people. Another was the local newspaper's reporter. The next day, the reporter came out to see what remained of the farm. The rubble still smoldered and the land was scorched, but he found Clarence in the field, hoeing and planting.

"I heard the awful news," he called to Clarence, "and I came out to do a story on the tragedy of your farm closing." Clarence just kept on hoeing and planting. The reporter kept prodding, kept poking, trying to get a rise from this quietly determined man who seemed to be planting instead of packing his bags. So, finally, the reporter said in a haughty voice, "Well, Dr. Jordan, you got two of them Ph.D.s and you've put fourteen years into this farm, and there's nothing left of it at all. Just how successful do you think you've been?"

Clarence stopped hoeing, turned toward the reporter with his penetrating blue eyes, and said quietly but firmly, "About as successful as the cross. Sir, I don't think you understand us. What we are about is not success but faithfulness. We're staying. Good day."

Beginning that day, Clarence and his companions rebuilt Koinonia and the farm is going strong today.[1]

Faithful to the gifts, abilities and opportunities God gives us

If we are faithful to the gifts, abilities and opportunities God gives us, we can leave the results to him. Take Moses, for example. He led God's people through good times and bad, and God considered him faithful. But one generation turned *from* God and one turned *to* God under Moses' leadership.

Was Moses more faithful the time they turned toward God? Probably not. It was not through Moses' failure that the first generation turned away or by his skill and success that the second turned to the Lord. Moses was simply faithful to God and what God had called him to do. As we just mentioned, when the New Testament speaks well of Moses saying he was "faithful in all God's house," it focuses on Moses faithfulness, not on what Moses accomplished. Faithfulness to the tasks God has given each of us is what God values.

Mother Teresa was a woman who understood God's faithfulness and being faithful to the task that was before her as her life's work. She also knew that God values faithfulness more than success:

Mark Hatfield tells of touring Calcutta with Mother Teresa and visiting the so-called "House of Dying," where sick children are cared for in their last days, and the dispensary, where the poor line up by the hundreds to receive medical attention. Watching Mother Teresa minister to these people, feeding and nursing those left by others to die, Hatfield was overwhelmed by the sheer magnitude of the suffering she and her co-workers face daily. "How can you bear the load without being crushed by it?" he asked. Mother Teresa replied, "My dear Senator, I am not called to be successful, I am called to be faithful."[2]

Faithfulness is when somebody has a word from God and stays true to it

John Wesley was an evangelist in England in the 1700's who was called to preach God's Word. In his diary, you can find these notations:

> May fifth, a.m., preached in Saint Anne's, was asked not to come back; p.m., preached at Saint John's, deacon said, "Get out, and stay out." May the 12th, preached at Saint Jude's, can't go back there; p.m. preached at Saint George, kicked out again. May the 29th preached at Saint Andrews, elders called a special meeting and said not to return; p.m. preached on the street and was run off. May 26, a.m., preached in a field, got chased by a bull that was set loose. June the 2nd a.m., preached at the edge of town, police moved me; p.m., preached in a pasture and ten thousand people came. [3]

Now what if Wesley had given up? What would have happened? What would have become of the multitudes of people that he led to Christ? Because he was faithful, even in the face of opposition, God used him. He became one of the greatest preachers of all time.

If you persevere in doing what God says, you can say along with Paul, "So, my dear brothers and sisters, be strong and immovable. Always work enthusiastically for the Lord, for you know that nothing you do for the Lord is ever useless" (1 Corinthians 15:58).

A faithful individual will not give up on another person

Faithful people believe the best in others. They have learned not to give up on others because they know God does not give up on them. Billy Graham is a faithful man of God who has preached the gospel for decades as an evangelist. There is no doubt that he is the kind of person who practices what he preaches.

In fact, this story of his prison visit to Jim Bakker, a TV evangelist convicted of fraud, gives us a glimpse into the character of the man. Although Jim ended up in prison where his duty was to clean out toilets, Billy visited him and treated him with respect even though Jim felt alone, lost, afraid and weak.

> When he came to visit me I had the flu. I looked like a man who had slept under a bridge. My hair was a mess and I had my old toilet-cleaning clothes on. My toes were sticking out of my shoes. I had just finished cleaning the toilets, and the guards came to get me. One of the guards led me across the compound, and I thought he was taking me to the lieutenant's office. I thought maybe I was in trouble. But then they said, "Didn't they tell you. Billy Gra-

ham is here to see you." So I walked into the room and he had his arms outstretched and he embraced me and told me he loved me. We sat and talked, and when he prayed everyone else in the room prayed. When you feel like you're worthless, and then somebody like that comes, it really is shocking.[4]

There is something beautiful about being able to see the potential in others, even when they've failed, and encourage them to go on with God. Remember our earlier definition of faithfulness? It means you can count on someone not to betray or desert you. This kind of faithfulness mirrors the faithfulness of God toward us.

God promotes faithful men and women

A faithful person does not give up. A faithful person sees something through the whole way to the end. The opposite of faithfulness is being a **Faithful people believe the best in others.** slothful person or a slacker. Proverbs 12:27 says that "Lazy people don't even cook the game they catch, the diligent make use of everything they find." Proverbs 18:9 says, "A lazy person is as bad as someone who destroys things." A slacker is someone who is afraid to step out in faith or in business because he is fearful of taking risks. He is "failure conscious" and thinks other people just hit lucky streaks. A lazy person has a victim mentality and accuses others for his lack of productiveness.

In the Parable of the Talents in the Bible, God spoke highly of the two servants who produced more from what they started with. "…Well done, my good and faithful servant. You have been faithful in handling this small amount, so now I will give you many more responsibilities…" (Matthew 25: 21). They demonstrated faithfulness to God, and God entrusted them with more.

But the third servant was not faithful. He hoarded his talent and did not increase it, therefore even that one talent was taken away from him. Notice that God was not evaluating the servants by the results they produced but by the faithfulness of their service.

God values faithfulness

As we show ourselves faithful in the small things God will open doors of promotion to us. Sometimes people are looking for open doors of opportunity and they're sitting around doing nothing. Faithfulness opens the door for new heights and promotions in your life.

Shortly after we were married, Sherlyn and I (Sam) moved to Phoenix, Arizona, for a couple of years. I worked in a hospital as an orderly for the radiology department. My job was to transport the patients by wheelchair or gurney from their rooms to get their x-rays taken. I faithfully did my job, but I didn't like it!

After about a year, I inquired about a job that would put me in charge of the orderlies. I decided that a job telling the other orderlies what to do would suit me perfectly. The supervisor informed me that I had to know how to type because there were requisitions to be typed up for that job position.

So I went to the library and got a book to learn how to type and went to Sears and bought myself a typewriter. I taught myself to type between 40 and 50 words a minute. Shortly thereafter, the position of supervising the orderlies opened up. I returned to my supervisor and asked for the job.

He said, "I told you before you have to be able to type." I told him I had taught myself to type and promptly typed out a letter to prove my skills. I got the job. Now I was the boss of the orderlies, and I liked that job a whole lot better.

Faithfulness is the key to promotion. Being reliable and faithful day-to-day—by being on time, keeping our commitments, being as good as our word—all adds up to being dependable and faithful. God says he will bless a faithful person: "A faithful man shall abound with blessings" (Proverbs 28:20 KJV).

As we show ourselves faithful in the small things God will open doors of promotion to us.

Faithfulness is constancy in the performance of our duties

A faithful person keeps his commitments, like arriving to work on time. Yes, getting to work in a consistent and timely fashion is connected to faithfulness! As faithful followers of Christ, we will complete the tasks God has given us to do.

To be faithful is to be consistent and reliable in our responsibilities. Can our friends and families and boss rely on us?

Faithfulness possesses a staying power in spite of feelings and difficulties. Think of anything—a new job, a new ministry assignment, a new marriage. At first there is a honeymoon and then it gets harder.

Faithfulness is hanging in there even after the first joy seems to disappear. 1 Corinthians 10:13 encourages us, "The temptations in your life are no different from what others experience. And God is faithful.

He will not allow the temptation to be more than you can stand. When you are tempted, he will show you a way out so that you can endure."

The faithfulness of God

In Lamentations, a beautiful picture of the faithfulness of God takes shape. It was a dark time in the history of God's people. Jerusalem had fallen to Babylon by the armies of King Nebuchadnezzar. Jerusalem's wall was breached and the city was looted and burned. The Temple was pulled down, and it seemed as though God's purposes had been entirely and utterly thwarted.

But here in the darkest of times, we find one of the greatest expressions of hope and God's unchanging love and faithfulness in the Bible. The prophet Jeremiah declares, "The faithful love of the Lord never ends! His mercies never cease. Great is his faithfulness; his mercies begin afresh each morning" (Lamentations 3:22-23).

God's love to us is constant and undeserved and guaranteed! It doesn't matter what the circumstances look like, or how we feel, or what we do—his love is unrelated to our performance (his mercies are new every day). "He is faithful to do what he says....and anyone who trusts in him will never be disgraced" (1 Corinthians 1:9; 1 Peter 2:6). Psalms 36:5 says, "Your unfailing love, O Lord, is as vast as the heavens; your faithfulness reaches beyond the clouds."

God, the faithful one, lives within us by the Holy Spirit. We can trust him to be completely faithful to us, and by his grace, we can produce a constant crop of faithfulness to him and to those he brings into our lives.

---

[1] Tim Hansel, *Holy Sweat*, (Waco, TX: Word Books Publisher, 1987), pp.188-189.
[2] Art Beals and Larry Libby, *Beyond Hunger*, (Kingsway Publications, 1987)
[3] Adapted from the Living Light Daily Devotional published by The Nationwide Christian Trust, http://www.hope-centre.com/hope%20times/AprMay08.pdf, accessed July 15, 2008.
[4] Adapted from: Christianity Today (12/7/98)

Fruit for Thought

1. How are you dependable? How have you been faithful to a word from God for your life?

2. Why does God value faithfulness more than success?

3. How have you been faithful in your relationships with others? How have you been faithful with your gifts and opportunities?

Chapter Ten

Gentleness

"Nothing is so strong as gentleness, nothing
so gentle as real strength."
Saint Francis de Sales

A 1960s television series entitled "Gentle Ben" starred a young boy, Mark, and his friendship and adventures with a 650-pound American black bear. The word *gentle* and *bear* might sound like an oxymoron, because when you think of a bear, you most likely think of a ferocious, man-eating animal on the prowl. Gentle Ben, however was a wild bear that had learned to yield to the will of his friend Mark. This gentle bear is an example of God's eighth exercise to become spiritually healthy—gentleness.

A couple of years ago, I (Sam) took my grandson to a Dude Ranch in Wyoming where they featured a horse whisperer. This cowboy, who had an unspoken rapport with horses, brought a wild bronco into the corral. The bronco started crashing against everything and anything trying to gain freedom. He tried to jump over the fence. He snorted and kicked and bucked. The horse whisperer stood still.

Slowly, he approached the bronco. At first, the bronco ran away high kicking and seemingly out of control. The man persisted. He patiently walked slowly and quietly after the horse and soon it started to calm down. Before long, it allowed the man to gently stroke its face and shoulder. In a short time, the bronco was following the man around!

I had seen other people breaking horses with whips and loud voices. I was struck with how superior this method was. The man continued his gentle ways and soon he was able to put a bridle on the horse, along with a blanket and saddle on his back. All this time, the man rubbed the horse's shoulder, quieting him. Before the end of one hour, he was on that wild bronco's back riding him gently around the corral. It was the first time this bronco had ever been ridden and he did not buck once! It was an amazing thing to behold. The bronco now actually looked meek.

Being gentle and meek is not a sign of weakness. It is strength that is harnessed.

Another word for *gentleness* could be the word *meekness*. Meekness is "strength under control." It is a state of being that puts complete trust in another. It is having a mild manner or disposition without needing to force its way. Being gentle and meek is not a sign of weakness. It is strength that is harnessed. It is the strength of God har-

Growing the Fruit of the Spirit

nessed in our lives for service to God. A wild bronco or wild bear does not lose any of its strength when it becomes tamed, but where they once had a will of their own, now they yield to the will of another.

A gentle person has a teachable spirit and puts his complete trust in the Lord. He stands strong and firm against the devil, and is compassionate and sees the best in people.

Gentle in our reaction to people and situations

The opposite of gentleness is self-assertiveness, self-interest or harshness. Do we jump to conclusions, before we understand the problem, causing us to react unsympathetically toward others? It's like the man who walked into a store and said, "Do you have anything to cure hiccups?" The shopkeeper promptly slapped him across the face.

"Hey, why'd you do that?" the man asked.

The shopkeeper smiled, "Well, you don't have hiccups anymore, do you?"

The man replied, "I never had the hiccups, I wanted something to cure my wife who is out in the car!"

An accurate definition of gentleness is "being considerate." When you think of a considerate person, they're thoughtful of the rights and feelings of others, and they don't rush to judgment. They don't start talking before they have the whole story. Gentleness takes the time to see the total picture before it reacts. It cares about people along the way and considers the emotional state of a person before responding.

In 1 Thessalonians 2:7 (NIV), Paul says, "As apostles of Christ...we were gentle among you, like a mother caring for her little children." Instead of using their authority to drive their message home, the apostles were gentle with the new Thessalonian believers.

The next time you eat at a restaurant, and your waiter confuses your order and spills coffee on your table, don't be so quick to complain. You don't know his life situation. You don't know what his morning was like before he arrived at work. If you have allowed God to grow gentleness in your life, you will react with compassion and gentleness to less than stellar service. Gentleness in the midst of a mess is a choice we make.

Gentleness takes the time to see the total picture before it reacts.

We live in a society where we are encouraged to get things done and get them done fast, even though people get hurt in the process. Success, accomplishment and productivity count, often at the expense of gentleness, kindness and being considerate.

Gentle in the words we speak

James 1:19 says, "...You must all be quick to listen, slow to speak, and slow to get angry." Maybe God gave us two ears and one mouth because we ought to listen twice as much as we talk! If we do the first two, the third is automatic. If you're quick to listen and if you're slow to speak you will be slow to anger.

Too often, we get things turned around. We are quick to speak, slow to listen, and swift to get angry. James goes on to say that "Human anger does not produce the righteousness God desires. So get rid of all the filth and evil in your lives, and humbly accept the word God has planted in your hearts, for it has the power to save your souls."

Proverbs 15:1 says that "a gentle answer deflects anger, but harsh words make tempers flare." How many times have we been in situations where we answered a harsh word with another harsh word, and a huge conflict ensues? Our words and even the tone of our words convey our gentle spirit, or lack thereof! Gentleness chooses to apologize.

Harsh words hurt. They hurt our children, they hurt our spouse, they hurt our friends, they even hurt our pets. Our little dog, Buffy is the gentlest little thing. When I (Sam) speak to her harshly because she misbehaves, she is visibly hurt and runs and cowers in a corner.

The Corinthian church was a church that spoke the right words but did not have the power to back them up. They were arrogant and lacking a gentle spirit. Paul gave the Corinthian church a choice: He could come to them and rebuke them or they could chose to submit to the Lord in love and the spirit of meekness.

"Some of you have become arrogant, thinking I will not visit you again. But I will come—and soon—if the Lord lets me, and then I'll find out whether these arrogant people just give pretentious speeches or whether they really have God's power. For the Kingdom of God is not just a lot of talk; it is living by God's power. Which do you choose? Should I come with a rod to punish you, or should I come with love and a gentle spirit?" (1 Corinthians 4:18-21).

Gentle in touch

When The Beatles sang "I Want to Hold Your Hand," little did they know that a scientific study some years later would show that physical contact improves people's health as well as their relationships. Researchers say that our bodies release a hormone called oxytocin when we're touched, and it interacts with dopamine, a brain chemical that makes us feel good. Oxytocin is one of those happy hormones that helps to lower blood pressure and stress levels, and can affect everything from how wounds heal to how much we trust other people.[1]

Gentle people have no problem touching others. As husbands, we love it when our wives slip their hands in ours when we are walking down the street or reach out with that tender touch as we sit together with them watching a movie. Touching brings life and healing to our lives. Jesus habitually touched someone when he healed them. Touching is meant to bring life.

Growing the Fruit of the Spirit

Gentle in restoration

All of us, at one time or another in our lives, has needed restoration. God wants us to be a healing and loving community that cares enough to restore someone who has fallen. Our goal as Christians is to help each other walk in the Spirit, not wait for someone to slip up and then pounce on them. If somebody is hurting, they need tenderness. They need somebody to apply a healing salve to the wound, not salt and vinegar.

Paul agrees, "...if another believer is overcome by some sin, you who are godly should gently and humbly help that person back onto the right path. And be careful not to fall into the same temptation yourself. Share each other's burdens, and in this way obey the law of Christ. If you think you are too important to help someone, you are only fooling yourself. You are not that important" (Galatians 6:1-3).

A gentle spirit is the result of realizing that we are what we are by the grace of God. We approach restoration with the attitude of being careful not to fall into the same temptation ourselves.

Moses was an individual in the Bible who exhibited gentleness and meekness even while under attack. In fact, the Bible says in Numbers 12 that he was the meekest man that ever lived. One time, his own sister and brother, Miriam and Aaron, criticized Moses because they were jealous. The Lord punished Miriam, the main instigator, by giving her leprosy. Moses, being the meek man that he was, did not look for revenge but instead pleaded with God to restore Miriam to health. Meekness is the character of someone who has the power to retaliate yet remains kind.

My (Sam) own father was a very gentle man. During my teenage years, I was rebellious and out doing my own thing. My father handled my rebellion so gently. I don't ever remember one argument we had. I wanted to have many arguments, but he never allowed me to engage him in one. Because my dad could control his actions and reactions to my bad behavior with his unconditional love and gentleness, I did not stray too far. His meekness kept me around God. I couldn't wander out there too far because I was witnessing a powerful character trait in my dad's gentleness.

Gentleness is a powerful force of God.

A gentle spirit is the result of realizing that we are what we are by the grace of God.

Jesus called himself the Good Shepherd which gives us a picture of one tenderly caring for his lambs. Jesus also speaks of his own gentleness when he said, "Take my yoke upon you. Let me teach you, because I am humble and gentle at heart, and you will find rest for your souls" (Matthew 11:29).

For generations, yokes have been placed over the shoulders of oxen so they could pull wagons or plow a field. The expectation was clear for the oxen that when the yoke was put over their shoulders, they were going to experience the burden of hard work.

We all have yokes, or expectations, so to speak, that we place on our lives. It is so important for us to allow Jesus to place his yoke on us, not our own yoke (our expectations) or the yoke of others (their expectations). The yoke of Jesus is gentle and light. He gives us the grace to do whatever he calls us to do. Jesus, the gentle one, lives within us. As we experience his gentleness each day, we will find ourselves being gentle to others around us.

[1] "The importance of touch" by Sharon Gray, http://www.eons.com/body/feature/mindspirit/the-importance-of-touch/17345, accessed May 22, 2008.

Fruit for Thought

1. How gentle are you in your reaction to people and situations?

2. Are you able to stand firm against the devil but compassionate toward others? Give an example.

3. Why is gentleness a powerful force of God?

Chapter Eleven

Self-Control

"Self-control is knowing when to say,
'that's enough for now.' We are desperate for
self-control, and in its absences, we are
drowning in self-defeat."
Beth Moore, *Living Beyond Yourself*

"Like a city whose walls are broken down is a
man who lacks self-control."
Proverbs 25:28

In the late 1960s, psychologist Walter Mischel launched what is often referred to as the "marshmallow experiment" that examined the processes that enable a young child to forego immediate gratification and to exert self-control. He left 4-year-olds in a room with a bell and a marshmallow. If they rang the bell, he would come back and they could eat the marshmallow. If, however, they didn't ring the bell and waited for him to come back in 15 minutes, they could then have two marshmallows.

In videos of the experiment, you can see the children squirming, kicking, hiding their eyes—desperately trying to exercise self-control so they can wait and get two marshmallows. Their performance varied widely. Some broke down and rang the bell within a minute. Others lasted 15 minutes.

Self-control is an essential character quality that God intends to grow inside of you.

Mischel followed the group and found that, 14 years later, those children who were able to exhibit self control and restrained themselves from taking the first marshmallow went on to become better adjusted children in later life.

They coped better socially and were more self assured of themselves. They had greater aptitude in academic studies, were more trustworthy and dependable. They also outperformed their counterparts in exams such as the SATs.

The children who rang the bell the quickest were more likely to become bullies. They received worse teacher and parental evaluations and were more likely to have drug problems.[1]

Long before the Mischel experiments, the Bible revealed that "self-control" is vital to our spiritual health. It is the ninth of the list of the fruit of the Spirit, and self-control is an essential character quality that God intends to grow inside of you. It is not unimportant that the fruit of the Spirit list in Galatians 5:22-23 begins with "love" and ends with "self-control." All of the rest of the fruit of the spirit...joy, peace, patience, kindness, goodness, faithfulness and gentleness fall in between *love* and *self-control*. It seems likely that if you develop "love" along with "self control" in your life, everything else begins to fall into place.

In all of your relationships it's important for love and self-control to remain in balance. You can't have one without the other. They cannot be independent of each other. You can't truly love without self-control and you can't have self-control without love.

When love and self-control cooperate together, they balance each other. When you have love and self-control in perspective, the other fruit of the Spirit are more easily cultivated. As a parent, a sister, a brother, a husband, a wife, or an employee, you realize that it is crucial that you love unconditionally and demonstrate self-control.

When love and self-control cooperate together, they balance each other.

When you are not motivated by love, you easily become frustrated, impatient and angry. When you are not self-controlled, you live with regret, wishing you could go back in time and undo your lack of self-control.

However, when you are motivated by love, you live beyond your expectations and realize you are capable of being patient, kind and joyful. When you have self-control, you realize you are equipped by the fruit of the Spirit to be gentle and peaceful even in the midst of difficult circumstances. In this fashion you become more like Christ and experience life beyond your own personal limitations.

What happens when your impulses are unchecked?

To have self-control means you have restraint over your impulses, emotions or desires. Living without restraint is like riding a roller coaster without brakes. It may be exciting initially as you streak down the tracks, but inevitably you'll pay a high price at the bottom.

As a teenager I (Sam) drove a dump truck for a company that put in sewage systems. One day, I was hauling a heavy truckload of stone and traveling down a hill. I started to engage the brakes only to discover that the pedal went the entire way to the floor board! I had no braking power! I quickly down-shifted but I was still going 30 miles per hour.

At the bottom of the hill was an intersection. I had no choice but to barrel through. Thankfully, it was a rural road with little traffic and no one was coming. I promptly maneuvered the truck off the road into a field and it finally came to a stop. I learned the hard way that if you lose your brakes you can be headed for disaster.

Likewise, if you disregard the brake of self-control in your life you may have some hard lessons to learn. Sometimes there may be only one area of your life that you don't have self-control in. You may think that it does not affect the rest of your life, but if it continues and you don't curb it and bring it under control, it could eventually affect your entire life.

Proverbs 25:28 tells us that if we lack self-control we are as defenseless as a city with broken-down walls. Consistent self-discipline will build up our spiritual defense system against the forces of evil.

Samson was a man who was set apart for God's service, but clearly lacked self-control in areas of his life. This lack of self-control eventually caused him to lose his way with God. Samson had a big problem with self-control when it came to his sexual appetite, and he also seems to have had serious anger management issues as well. In the course of his life, he allowed two women to seduce him, particularly Delilah, who caused him to lose God's anointing on his life.

If you disregard the brake of self-control in your life you may have some hard lessons to learn.

Several times he took excessive revenge—once by murdering 30 innocent men to obtain their coats to pay a debt he owed. Anger, revenge and lust characterized his life because he failed to check the impulses that began early in his life. Those unchecked impulses eventually killed him (Judges 13-16).

Where you need self-control

You need self-control to control your words, your food intake, your shopping, your spending, your thoughts, your physical desires, and the list goes on. All those desires are not wrong. The problem comes when you surrender yourself indiscriminately to your desires and appetites. Paul wrote in 1 Corinthians 10:23, "You say, 'I am allowed to do anything'—but not everything is good for you...."

Dieters will say, "Next time you want a cupcake, eat a carrot." When we discipline ourselves to keep our ordinary desires under control, we practice the reality of Paul's words in Romans 6:18, "Now you are free from your slavery to sin, and you have become slaves to righteous living."

Self-control means restraining your impulses, emotions, appetites and desires. You think that giving in to your desires will satisfy you, but very often the reverse is true. Eating a whole bag of potato chips may give you pleasure for a short while but most likely you will soon feel miserable and undisciplined.

God doesn't expect you to completely deprive yourself of every desire you have. Instead, you satisfy the desires that God has given you in appropriate ways. For example:

> We deny ourselves, we control ourselves, because we love Christ and we want to please Him. We master our desires in order to worship Him. Food is His gift; we eat in moderation with thankfulness to gain strength to serve Him. Rest is His gift; we rest, not in idle self-indulgence, but so that we may be refreshed to serve Him.

Sex is His gift; we use it to serve Him in becoming one with our spouse in marriage and in practicing chastity outside of marriage.

We master our desires, our time, our thoughts, our desire for nice things–all in order that we might offer all we are and all we have to Him as acts of worship. The self-control that is the fruit of the Spirit is not control by me or for me. It is not my going on a diet because summer is coming and I want to look better in my bathing suit. That is not the fruit of the Spirit. The fruit of the Spirit is submitting our desires and our opportunities to Christ.[2]

Some people seem to think that self-control makes you rigid. Just the opposite is true. It actually makes you resilient. It increases your capacity to be courageous when life gets tough or be disciplined when you feel yourself going out of control. When life gets tough and you're not disciplined you will quit, but a disciplined person will press on.

Self-control is to do what you do not want to do when you do not want to do it because you have to do it.

Someone once said that self-control is to do what you do not want to do when you do not want to do it because you have to do it. This is a pretty good definition. The Bible tells us, "I discipline my body like an athlete, training it to do what it should. Otherwise,

I fear that after preaching to others I myself might be disqualified" (1 Corinthians 9:27).

How do you develop self-control?

You develop self-control by building disciplines into your life. Paul said in 1 Corinthians 9 that in a race everyone runs but only one person gets the prize. So we should run to win. In order to win, athletes must be disciplined in their training. Self-control needs a goal! The prize, the goal, provides focus. The reason so many of us do not exercise self-control is because we do not have a goal. There is no motivation to discipline ourselves.

Did you ever notice that you should not go grocery shopping when you are hungry? You tend to pick up a lot more items than you intended, because your stomach tells you it needs almost everything it sees! It requires self-control to remind yourself what is important to buy and what is not.

We both travel all over the world and at times need to eat all kinds of food, but we are local country boys at heart who love good old Lancaster County Pennsylvania Dutch home cooking. And whoopie pies, those delicious freshly baked chocolate cookies and crème delicacies, are near the top of the list!

I (Sam) was recently at the grocery store buying things on my list. As I headed for the checkout counter, I glanced at a package of four whoopie pies. My stomach started rumbling for those lovely Pennsylvania Dutch chocolate cookies with thick frosting in between! I hastily added them to my cart. Before I left the grocery store's parking lot, I had eaten one.

It was about 3:00 clock in the afternoon and I hadn't had much to eat that day. So, I realized I was really hungry. I ate another whoopie pie and then another. That one remaining cookie looked so lonely in the package. If I ate it, no one would ever know that I had eaten any whoopie pies at all! There would be no incriminating partial package. So I ate the final, and fourth, whoopie pie. *Can you believe Sam ate a whole package of whoopie pies? I can. Because I (Larry) have gone on similar binge eating sprees! Let's admit it, most of us have done it!*

The solution to having self-control is not trying to do it on our own. Instead, we desperately need God's power and grace.

The next day I was upset with myself. Why had I given in to all those calories when I really didn't need them? I had a goal of losing weight, not gaining it! That day, I disciplined my body by doing not one, but two, workouts. I knew I had to bring my eating habits under control.

Some of the best scriptures on self-control in the New Testament are in Titus 2. Titus was the church leader on the island of Crete which was known as a "party place." Paul describes the people who lived there as "liars, cruel animals, and lazy gluttons" (Titus 1:12). It probably was not an easy place for Christians to maintain their self-control.

Paul challenges the church, including both the older and younger men and women, to be "in their right minds" by being controlled by the Spirit. He goes on to remark that the solution to having self-control is not about us trying to do it on our own. Instead, we desperately need God's power and grace.

"For the grace of God that brings salvation has appeared to all men. It teaches us to say 'No' to ungodliness and worldly passions, and to live self-controlled, upright and godly lives in this present age while we wait for the blessed hope—the glorious appearing of our great God and Savior, Jesus Christ, who gave himself for us to redeem us from all wickedness and to purify for himself a people that are his very own, eager to do what is good" (Titus 2:11-14 NIV).

Notice the emphasis on "grace." That's how we develop self-control. Grace not only redeems us (verses 11-14), it reforms us (verses 12-14). Because of Jesus, we are not only forgiven, but we've also been given a change in attitude and desires. We are free from sin's weight on our lives. It is the Spirit who works new life in us and helps us to overcome. It is the work of the Spirit and the grace of God that helps us develop self-control; we can't do it on our own.

Years ago, I (Larry) received a revelation from the Lord about the grace of God that has literally revolutionized my life. Although I was in love with Jesus and filled with the Holy Spirit, I felt like I was living in a mental prison. It seemed like some things would never change.

Then one day someone vividly described the "grace of God" to me in a way that literally changed my life! I learned that grace is God's unimaginable and total kindness! We receive it freely and do not deserve it, and our hearts cannot but change because of it. We cannot fully describe it, but we can experience it.

Grace affects everything we do in life. When I finally began to understand the grace of God, it changed the way I thought, acted and responded to difficulties that arose in my life.

Grace is sometimes defined as *the free unmerited favor of God on the undeserving and ill-deserving.* We cannot earn it; it is a gift. For example, our salvation comes as a gift of God's grace, and it can be accessed by our response of faith. Grace could be described as a coin with two distinct sides to it. We just described the one side of the coin that is characterized by the saving grace of God— "the free unmerited favor of God on the undeserving and ill-deserving." The other side of the grace coin is the grace God gives to believers to give them the "desire and the power to do God's will." He gives us the desire and power to do his will, including experiencing the fruit of self-control in our lives by his grace!

One of the chores I really disliked growing up as a farm boy was herding pigs. You may have heard of the terminology that someone is "pig-headed." In other words, they have a mind of their own and do not like to take orders from anyone. Well, the term pig-headed comes from the strong will that pigs have. Whenever I had to chase pigs, I would get so angry at them because they always wanted to go everywhere except where I was trying to herd them! I was convinced that demons were still living in pigs today, leftover from the time in the Bible when Jesus cast the demons out of the Gadarene demoniac into the herd of hogs!

"For the grace of God that brings salvation...teaches us to live self-controlled..."
Titus 2:11

One day while lunging and yelling and stomping after the pigs, I realized I was in desperate need of self-control. I found that these pigs were controlling my emotions and robbing me of righteousness, peace and joy in the Holy Spirit! Then it hit me. The reality is that Christ lives in me and he is the ultimate example of self-control. I realized that I could not work up self control in my own ability, but by the grace of God, I could release the fruit of self-control in my life. And it worked! It wasn't me, but Christ in me giving me the grace to experience self-control. I literally ran around the barnyard chasing stubborn, squealing pigs telling myself that I was self-controlled, in Jesus' name. And I was!

Building vision in your life helps you to be disciplined

The Bible says that when you have no aim in life, when you have no boundaries, you run wild and lack self-control. "Where there is no vision, the people are unrestrained…" (Proverbs 29:18 NAS). Moses, when he became of age, refused to be called the son of Pharaoh's daughter, choosing rather to suffer affliction with the people of God than to enjoy the luxury and pleasures of royalty. He chose the disciplined path that God had prepared for him, and he became one of the greatest leaders in history.

The disciplined path means you must live intentionally. Henry David Thoreau said, "In the long run men hit only what they aim at." You need to implement daily goals in your life that give you direction. Be a person that commits yourself to regular evaluations on how you are doing with respect to your goals in life.

Paul said, "I have fought a good fight, I have finished my course." Notice that Paul says "my course." He was speaking of the particular course that had been assigned to him. There was the particular purpose God had for his life, and he was running the course that God had given him. We all have a purpose in life, a destiny that God wants us to fulfill.

Discover the plan God has for you—a plan for living out your God-given purpose and calling. Trust him to give you the discipline and self-control to stay focused on the plan he has for you. It all starts with exercising the fruit of self-control by taking the first step.

[1] "Self-control is the key to success," by David Brooks, New York Times Service, Tuesday, May 9, 2006, http://www.sfgate.com/cgi-bin/article.cgi?f=/c/a/2006/05/09/EDGFGINST41.DTL&hw=david+brooks&sn=002&sc=613, accessed May 26, 2008.

[2] Jim Meek, *Like a City Without Walls: Self-Control and the Fruit of the Spirit*, http://www.covenantseminary.edu/resource/Meek_LikeACity.pdf, accessed June 6, 2008.

Fruit for Thought

1. Describe a time you gave in to an impulse.

2. What happens when your impulses go unchecked?

3. What efforts are you making to develop self-control? How does grace factor in?

Chapter Twelve

Growing Spirit Fruit

"God wants spiritual fruit,
not religious nuts."
Unknown

A story is told of two brothers who were sent to their room because they had been bad. But the punishment was never very effective, because they learned that they could climb out their window, onto the roof, and down a large old fruit tree. From there they would run across the back yard, over the fence, and into the fields, where they would play ball. Then they returned to their room, and no one ever knew they were gone.

One day they overheard Dad saying to Mom, "That old tree hasn't borne fruit for years. Tomorrow morning I'm going to cut it down." They were horrified. They needed a plan. They gathered together all of their money and bought all of the apples they could find, along with some string. Late that night, they proceeded to tie apples onto every branch of that old tree that they could reach. Then they went to bed and waited for their dad to get up in the morning.

The next morning their dad saw the apple-laden tree and burst back into the house, "It's the most incredible thing I've ever seen! This tree which hasn't borne fruit for years is covered with apples! You have to see this: it is absolutely covered with big, red, juicy apples! I don't believe it! It's a pear tree!"

Yes, it is a fact of nature that apples grow on apple trees and pear trees produce pears. The kind of fruit that grows on the outside is a reflection of the nature of the tree. Likewise, the fruit of the Spirit that grows in your life is an outgrowth of the nature within. It is the nature of God growing within you which expresses itself in the kind of fruit that grows on the outside.

You are the work of God's hand. He has planted you and anticipates that you will grow spiritual fruit in his productive vineyard. There is a powerful story in the Bible that bears this out. It is an acted-out, living parable that Jesus performed to teach his disciples this important truth.

One day Jesus was strolling down Bethany Road to the city of Jerusalem. He saw the leaves of a fig tree in the distance and, since he was hungry, he looked forward to eating some of its fresh figs. However, when he arrived at the tree he discovered that it had no fruit. It was all leaves and no fruit. He cursed the tree saying, "May no fruit ever come from you again!" (Matthew 21:19; Mark 11:14). The tree immediately withered up and died.

The withered fig tree is a dramatic "visual aid" to a truth Jesus intended to illustrate. Although scholars have different opinions about the exact lesson to be taught, we tend to believe that Jesus' cursing of the fig tree demonstrated that God will judge those who give an outer appearance of fruitfulness but in fact are not fruitful at all.

The fruit of the Spirit that grows in your life is an outgrowth of the nature within.

The fig tree had leaves on it. It appeared to have the outward signs of productivity. But upon closer examination it became clear it was only a pretense.

If professed followers of Jesus practice only a form and outward performance of religion rather than having their confidence and faith in him, they are "talking the talk" but not "walking the walk." The lesson of the fig tree is that we should bear spiritual fruit (Galatians 5:22-23), not just give an appearance of religiosity. God judges fruitlessness, and expects that those who have a relationship with him will "bear much fruit" (John 15:5-8).

As Christians we are to bear the fruit of the Spirit. If these fruit are not manifested in our lives, we will eventually be judged. A question we must all ask ourselves is this: "What fruit am I bearing for the Lord?"

Like the fig tree, our purpose for existing is to bear fruit. When the fig tree was no longer fulfilling its purpose, it withered away. Believers also can wither away spiritually. Trials in our lives will either cause us to bear spiritual fruit, or keep us from being fruitful. It depends on how we respond to the tests.

You probably know by now that just trying harder doesn't work! You can try and try to be patient, or try and try to be filled with joy, but without the Spirit your efforts are fruitless. Fruit comes by knowing we are connected to the vine (Jesus) and allowing him to grow the fruit in our lives. Let's look at a few keys to growing fruit.

1. Realize that Christ lives in you

While you may have some responsibility for your spiritual growth, it is really the work of Christ that gives impetus to your life. It is only by Christ living within you that you have the power to bear spiritual fruit.

When you placed your faith in Christ, Christ came to dwell within you by means of the Holy Spirit (Romans 8:9). His purpose for dwelling in you is that he might live his life through you. You should never try to operate on your own finite ability but instead in Christ's infinite power. "My old self has been crucified with Christ. It is no longer I who live, but Christ lives in me. So I live in this earthly body by trusting in the Son of God, who loved me and gave himself for me" (Galatians 2:20).

2. Stay attached to the Vine!

The Bible teaches us that our spiritual life will falter if we don't actively remain in Christ and produce fruit. "Remain in me, and I will remain in you. For a branch cannot produce fruit if it is severed from the vine, and you cannot be fruitful unless you remain in me" (John 15:4).

That's all we have to do. Remain attached to Jesus. He does the work. A couple of years ago, the Associated Press released a study done by an agricultural school in Iowa. It reported that production of 100 bushels of corn from one acre of land, in addition to the many hours of the farmer's labor, required 4,000,000 pounds of water, 6,800 pounds of oxygen, 5,200 pounds of carbon, 160 pounds of nitrogen, 125 pounds of potassium, 75 pounds of yellow sulfur, and other elements too numerous to list.

In addition to these things, which no man can produce, rain and sunshine at the right time are critical. It was estimated that only 5% of the produce of a farm can be attributed to the efforts of man. If we were honest, we'd have to admit that the same is true in producing spiritual fruit.

In fact, the next verse bears this out, "...Those who remain in me, and I in them, will produce much fruit. For apart from me you can do nothing" (John 15: 5). As the branches remain firmly attached to the vine, they just naturally bear fruit. No work, no strain, no sweat. We bear fruit effortlessly only by remaining attached to Christ. As we hang tight to the Vine, he does the growing!

A veteran missionary had served the Lord for many years in China. One day he found himself taking a walk in a park pondering what he had accomplished in the past years. His attention was drawn to a tree with one particularly large branch growing from its trunk. God spoke to the missionary, "What is that large branch doing?" The missionary had to admit, "It is just staying attached to the trunk." And then he realized that that is exactly what the Lord wanted him to continue to do. Only by remaining attached would he bear fruit.

3. We must learn to embrace the greenhouse (trials)

Trees and crops need fertilizer. In fact, one of the best fertilizers is manure. It smells bad but it works in the long run. Sometimes things happen in our lives that just smell bad! We need to look at them as God's fertilizer that will help us produce good fruit. Remember what James 1:2-4 says: "When troubles come your way, consider it an opportunity for great joy. For you know that when your faith is tested, your endurance has a chance to grow. So let it grow, for when your endurance is fully developed, you will be perfect and complete, needing nothing."

Regardless of why these tests come, God will use them in our lives to produce spiritual fruit if we trust him. The tests that come may try to keep us from bearing spiritual fruit, but if we respond properly to these trials, they will increase the fruit in our lives. Don't waste your trials. Remember, when you are enrolled in God's school of life, he will give tests. But no matter how many times you fail the test, you will not get kicked out of his school. He will just continue to give you the tests until you pass!

4. The Lord may need to prune good things from our lives

My (Larry) parents radically prune their chrysanthemums every year, leaving only a few sprigs. But those sprigs produce sturdy, full plants in due time. When grapes are pruned, the master gardener cuts away close to ninety percent of the growth leaving only one shoot. But that shoot generates multiple shoots and yields luscious grapes.

In short, pruning improves a plant's health and strength and encourages new growth. Spiritually, God prunes us in an effort to change us. Though painful, pruning will help us to grow stronger. Sometimes we think that God only prunes us of sinful behavior—dead wood that needs to be cut away. But that is not always the case. He also cuts things off things even in those areas where we are healthy, just as we prune a healthy plant to stimulate growth and greater fruitfulness.

Many years ago, as a young leader, a trusted leader and friend spoke prophetically into my life that there was a time of pruning coming to our church. It came, and it was painful. Good leaders I served with left. Only later, did I realize it was the best thing that could have happened to me. I believe God cut away a lot of what I held dear so that the only shoot that remained was God and

God alone. Pruning hurts. And even though we will bear more fruit later, the pruning time feels like God has abandoned us. But he hasn't. He cares about us and wants us to bear much fruit. He wants to free us from the branches that drain our life and energy, and only he knows us well enough to know which branches to cut out.

Although it is not pleasant, pruning is absolutely essential for spiritual growth. God holds the cutting shears, and he knows what he is doing.

5. Resist the enemy and the old nature

When you receive Christ you receive a new nature inside—the nature of God himself which include the characteristics of love, joy, peace, patience, kindness, goodness, faithfulness, gentleness and self-control. But your old, sinful nature also remains even after you come to faith in Christ. The new nature and the old nature remain with you side by side, with the old nature being your enemy. We must resist and put to death our sinful nature through continual spiritual warfare that you wage through the power of the Holy Spirit. In this way you destroy sin's power and walk in fellowship with God.

Spiritually, God prunes us in an effort to change us.

"Those who belong to Christ Jesus have nailed the passions and desires of their sinful nature to his cross and crucified them there. Since we are living by the Spirit, let us follow the Spirit's leading in every part of our lives" (Galatians 5:24-25).

6. Put on your new nature

Colossians 3:10 says, "Put on your new nature, and be renewed as you learn to know your Creator and become like him." That little phrase "put on" speaks volumes. You must *put on* your new nature. A coat hanging in the closet does you no good until you put it on. It's the same way with the nature of God.

How do you "put on" or "wear" your new nature? How do you change your moral clothes? God doesn't just say you should get rid of your old habits and get new ones as you work hard to improve and change yourself. Instead, God creates the new person that you must put on. God creates the new you. He gives you the assignment to become holy, but he is the one who creates your holiness. So it is all by his grace that you can do anything.

The world is looking for the character of God to be exhibited in the lives of Christians. The Bible teaches that whatever we sow we will also reap (Galatians 6:7). When you sow the fruit of the Spirit into the lives of others, you will also reap the same fruit from others in the future.

7. Growing fruit takes time

We both grew up on farms. Farmers learn quickly that it takes months to produce a crop, and some plants take years before they produce fruit. It can get pretty frustrating if you think you will see growth by staring at a field of dirt with some seeds in it. You could stand there for days without seeing any growth. But eventually what is happening beneath the surface is displayed in a fresh shoot of new green growth breaking the surface of the soil.

Although it seemed as though nothing was changing because you were watching for growth from a constant, up-close perspective, the changes taking place are really drastic once they come to the surface. From a spiritual standpoint, look at your life: where are you now compared to ten years ago? When you look at it like that, from a larger perspective, you see the drastic growth.

The Bible says, "Dear brothers and sisters, be patient as you wait for the Lord's return. Consider the farmers who patiently wait for the rains in the fall and in the spring. They eagerly look for the valuable harvest to ripen" (James 5:7).

Farmers know that patience is vital when it comes to seeing results and growth. In due time they can expect the harvest to be ripened, but they cannot hurry it. They can't control the rain, the sun or the season. Likewise, we can't control and hasten the events in our lives that God alone is in control of. We must be patient for him to develop the fruit in us.

John Wesley had been an Anglican priest and a missionary to the Native Americans and colonists in Georgia; however he didn't have peace about his own destiny. He constantly wondered if he was right with God. In the midst of a devastating storm between England and Georgia, Wesley was deeply impressed by a group of Moravians who remained calm by singing hymns. The fruit of the Spirit he witnessed in their lives led him to a genuine con-

Patience is vital when it comes to seeing results and growth.

version experience which deeply affected his personal life and theology and millions of others who he influenced.

Are you a fruit inspector?

We are not called to judge other Christians. If their fruit fails to measure up to our standards it is not up to us to monitor their behavior and pass judgment on them. On a tree, all of the fruit is not ripe at the same time and it is not all of the same quality. Some may have spots from disease or bruises from a recent pelting rain.

Christians, too, are at different stages of development. Someone may have just come through difficult circumstances that places stress on the fruit. If we look at the whole picture and discern the season they are in, we will not be so quick to criticize.

However, we need to be fruit inspectors in the aspect of discerning truth from error. Matthew 7 says that we are not to believe everything someone says just because they say they are Christians. If someone's fruit is altogether and wholly rotten, we know that he or she is not walking with God.

Matthew 7:15-20 says, "Beware of false prophets who come disguised as harmless sheep but are really vicious wolves. You can identify them by their fruit, that is, by the way they act. Can you pick grapes from thorn bushes, or figs from thistles? A good tree produces good fruit, and a bad tree produces bad fruit. A good tree can't produce bad fruit, and a bad tree can't produce good fruit. So every tree that does not produce good fruit is chopped down and thrown into the fire. Yes, just as you can identify a tree by its fruit, so you can identify people by their actions."

Luke 6:43-45 says it similarly, "A good tree can't produce bad fruit, and a bad tree can't produce good fruit. A tree is identified by its fruit. Figs are never gathered from thorn bushes, and grapes are not picked from bramble bushes. A good person produces good things from the treasury of a good heart, and an evil person produces evil things from the treasury of an evil heart. What you say flows from what is in your heart."

What is down deep in a person's roots produces the eventual fruit. Roots produce fruit!

What does your fruit taste like?

Let's take the fruit test. If we are not bearing good spiritual fruit in our lives, we need to repent and receive grace from the Lord to begin to show evidence of love, joy, peace, patience, kindness, goodness, faithfulness, gentleness, and self-control.

What do people taste when they take a bite out of us? We must ask ourselves, do we have the fruit of the Spirit growing from our lives? People around us have an expectation that if we are believers in Jesus, there will be fruit in our lives.

Our God is the God of another chance! Jesus told this story: "A man planted a fig tree in his garden and came again and again to see if there was any fruit on it, but he was always disappointed. Finally, he said to his gardener, 'I've waited three years, and there hasn't been a single fig! Cut it down. It's just taking up space in the garden.'

"The gardener answered, 'Sir, give it one more chance. Leave it another year, and I'll give it special attention and plenty of fertilizer. If we get figs next year, fine. If not, then you can cut it down'" (Luke 13:6-9).

Has God showed you an area of your life where fruit is missing or needs maturing? He is giving you another chance to grow spiritual fruit! God is a merciful God who grants time and resources to help us repent where we have missed it and walk in his grace each day. "The life of the Christian disciple is to be characterized by continual, daily repentance and renewal. Each day is a day of grace, allowing a fresh opportunity for repentance and a renewed life of discipleship, living out the fruits of repentance."[1]

Put your spiritual health as a high priority and ask yourself, "Am I staying fit and healthy spiritually by exercising the fruit of the Spirit in my life?" You will affect your spiritual health daily by the choices you make.

You have the wonderful virtues of godly character as the result of God's Spirit acting from within you. Bear much fruit and give yourselves to others. The fruit is manifested in relationships. God's Spirit is like a river (John 7:38). It will flow *into* us only when it is also flowing *out* to others. Choose to incorporate the fruit of the Spirit, God's nine exercises to spiritual health, into your life minute by minute. Remember, love is the key.

Am I staying fit and healthy spiritually by exercising the fruit of the Spirit in my life?

> Love is the key. Joy is love singing. Peace is love resting. Patience is love enduring. Kindness is love's touch. Goodness is love's character. Faithfulness is love's habit. Gentleness is love's self-forgetfulness. Self-control is love holding the reins."[2]

Christ lives in you; he has given you the power and the grace to produce lots of good fruit!

[1] Hultgren, Arland J., *The Parables of Jesus*, (Grand Rapids, MI: William B. Eerdman's Publishing Company, 2000), p 246.
[2] D.G. Barnhouse, www.alliancenet.org/ barnhouse, accessed July 2008.

Fruit for Thought

1. What are you doing to stay attached to the Vine?

2. Describe a time the Lord has needed to prune something from your life.

3. What do people taste when they take a bite out of your spiritual fruit?

Love

1. Love produced by the action of the Holy Spirit

a. The Greek word for this kind of love is *agape*. It is unconditional love that is the unearned love God has for humanity.

b. God demonstrated his limitless love when he gave his only son who lay down his life at the cross (John 15:13).

c. Love without expecting to receive anything in return.

Ex: Daughter who loved her dad with no expectancy of the love being reciprocated.

2. It's a love with a commitment to care about others

a. It's a love that is willing to "lay down our lives for others" (1 John 7-8)

Ex: Brother who was willing to die for his sister who needed a blood transfusion.

b. It is a love that is extravagant and sacrificial.

3. How love grows

a. Read the Love Chapter (1 Corinthians 13).

b. Love is not a feeling, but a decision.

c. God fills our hearts, and love grows (Romans 5:5; Philippians 1:9).

4. Love calls us to each other

a. Love opens the way to a life of fruitfulness and spiritual productivity—and spills out to those around you.

Ex: "Tonight I gave my love away."—Mary Martin

b. Acts 9: Story of Dorcas is not about what she said, but about what she *did* for others.

c. How have you loved others beyond your human capability?

Teaching Outlines
Chapter 4

Joy

1. **Joy is "cheerfulness or a calm delight"**
   a. Joy is an orientation of the heart, not dependent on circumstances.

   Ex: Son killed in auto accident.

   b. How often did you laugh this week?

2. **Joy changes our spiritual climate**
   a. It changes the way we perceive our circumstances.
   b. Joy and worshiping go hand-in-hand

3. **Jesus is a joy bringer**
   a. Jesus lived one hundred percent in the Father's will, showing us what God is really like.
   b. Even from the beginning of time, Jesus rejoiced in the presence of a joyful God: "I was his constant delight, rejoicing always in his presence" (Proverbs 8:22-31).

4. **Jesus pours his capacity for joy into us**
   a. He wants our joy to be full (John 15:11).
   b. Jesus' followers rejoiced even in prison (Acts 16).

5. **Joy brings strength into circumstances and opens doors for you**
   a. Nehemiah 8:10 - "The joy of the Lord is your strength!"
   b. Acts 16 - doors of prison were opened

6. **Consider it joy when you face trials (James 1:2-5)**
   a. God can use trials to work his character in our lives.
   b. Celebrate life today. Jump for joy! (Psalm 16:11)

Peace

1. Peace is "freedom from agitation or disturbance"
a. A branch does not bear fruit by struggling.
b. The kind of peace Jesus gives (Philippians 4:7; Romans 15:13).

2. Peace allows us to hear God more clearly
a. Peace is an inner-knowing that our actions are approved by God (Colossians 3:15; Philippians 4:6-7).
b. Give your worries to God (1 Peter 5:7) and pray instead.

3. Peace brings rest and confidence in God
a. The story of Daniel in the lions' den is an account of placing one's complete trust in God.
b. How has peace in your heart enabled you to hear from God more clearly?

4. Living life with purpose brings peace
a. God's peace comes from a purpose focused on God and others.
b. Sow seeds of encouragement into someone's life.

5. Be a peacemaker
a. Living in the peace of God is being clothed with the powerful character of Christ.
b. Work for peace (Matthew 5:9).
c. How have you been a peacemaker?

Patience

1. **Patience is "a quality of self-restraint in the face of provocation"**
   a. It is waiting long for justice.
   b. It is bearing trials calmly or without complaint.

2. **Patience is not letting go of your dream from God**
   a. We wait patiently on the Lord, all the while being fully convinced of his faithful timing (Habakkuk 2:1-3).

   Ex: Woman waiting for a future husband.
   b. Describe how patience was "not letting go of your dream from God."

3. **Patience in our interaction with people**
   a. Day-to-day patience involves making allowance for others' faults (Colossians 3:12-13).

   Ex: Man on train with baby

4. **Patience is a powerful character builder**
   a. When your faith is tested, it grows patience (James 1:1-4).
   b. Relax and enjoy the wait in God's "waiting room" by allowing the fruit of his patience to flow through you!
   c. How do you react when God is not moving as quickly as you want?

Kindness

1. Clothe yourself with kindness (Colossians 3:12,14)

   a. Like all the fruit, kindness is in you in seed form when you become a believer and are made holy.

   b. The action part is for you to put them on (clothe yourself—develop them).

2. Kindness reaches out

   a. Kindness is the opposite of self-centeredness (Philippians 2:3-4).

   Ex: Grouchy, elderly man was shown kindness by clerks in a grocery store. He left them money from his estate.

   b. How do you encourage and affirm people?

3. Kindness is appreciating differences

   a. Try to understand others' viewpoints.

   Ex: In restaurant, find opportunities to be considerate instead of demanding.

4. Kindness is doing good when you feel you have a right to retaliate

   a. God revealed his kindness and love and saved us even though we were foolish and disobedient (Titus 3:3-5).

   b. God wants us to express this kindness to our fellow man (Luke 6:27-31), even enemies!

   c. Have you ever felt you had the right to retaliate but instead "turned the other cheek"?

Goodness

1. Goodness often expresses itself in deeds
Ex: Good Samaritan, George Washington Carver
a. Goodness is love in action!

2. Goodness goes hand-in-hand with the love we have for our fellowman and kindness we show
a. Goodness comes from a place in our hearts, but it always requires action.
b. Have you been generous and shown mercy to others?

3. The source of goodness
a. Jesus said only God is truly good (Mark 10:17-18).
b. Goodness is not natural to the human heart.
c. Only God's goodness is absolute. We merely have degrees of goodness as measured against this absolute standard.

4. What does goodness require?
a. Micah 6:8 tells us: "to do what is right, to love mercy, and to walk humbly with your God."
b. We look at God's goodness and respond by showing justice, mercy and humility. We act toward God and others according to God's divine standard of righteousness.
c. Describe how you have shown goodness to someone who has sinned against you.

Faithfulness

1. **Faithfulness is "reliability, trustworthiness, steadfast-ness"**
   a. When you think of a faithful person, who comes to your mind?

2. **God is looking for faithful people**
   a. Faithful people understand the reality of commitment, and persevere when the going gets tough (Proverbs 20:6).
   b. Why did God consider Moses faithful? (Hebrews 3:2).

3. **Be faithful to the gifts and opportunities God gives**
   a. God focuses on our faithfulness, not on what we accomplish.

4. **A faithful individual will not give up on another person**
   a. Faithful people believe the potential in others even when they failed.

5. **God promotes faithful people**
   a. In the Parable of the Talents (Matthew 25:21), God spoke highly of the two servants who produced more from what they started with.
   b. They demonstrated faithfulness to God, and God entrusted them with more.

6. **God values faithfulness**
   a. Read Proverbs 28:20.
   b. God is faithful (Lamentations 3:22-23).
   c. How have you been faithful in your relationships with others? With your gifts and opportunities?

Gentleness

1. Gentleness is "strength under control"

Ex: Wild bronco and horse whisperer.

a. Gentleness is the strength of God being harnessed in our lives for service to him.

b. A gentle person has a teachable spirit.

2. We must be gentle in our reaction to people and situations

a. The opposite of gentleness is self-assertiveness and self-interest.

b. We are thoughtful of the rights and feelings of others (1 Thessalonians 2:7).

3. We are gentle in the words we speak

a. James 1:19 says we should be quick to listen, slow to speak and slow to get angry.

b. Proverbs 15:1 says a gentle answer deflects anger.

4. We should be gentle in touch

Ex: Physical contact improves people's health. Bodies release hormones that make us feel good.

5. We must be gentle in restoration

a. We all need restoration at points in our lives. God wants us to be a healing and loving community that cares enough to restore someone who has fallen.

b. Why is gentleness such a powerful force of God?

Self-Control

1. **Self-control is a vital character quality for life**

   Ex: Mischel experiment

2. **When love and self-control cooperate, they balance each other**

   a. The fruit of the Spirit starts with "love" and ends with "self-control." You can't have one without the other.

3. **What happens when your impulses are unchecked?**

   a. Proverbs 25:28 says if we lack self-control we are as defenseless as a city with broken-down walls.

   b. Samson was a man who lacked self-control which eventually caused him to lose his way with God.

4. **Where you need self-control**

   a. In everything! Desires are not wrong, but to surrender yourself indiscriminately to your appetites is (1 Corinthians 10:23).

   b. Self-control does not make you rigid, it makes you resilient. It increases your capacity to be courageous when life gets tough or be disciplined when you feel yourself going out of control.

5. **How do you develop self-control?**

   a. You build disciplines in your life (1 Corinthians 9).

   b. You are controlled by the Spirit and walk in God's grace (Titus 2:11).

   c. Build vision in your life to help you be disciplined. Live intentionally.

   d. What efforts are you making to develop self-control? How does grace factor in?

About the Authors

Larry Kreider is the founder and International Director of DOVE Christian Fellowship International (DCFI), an international family of churches that has successfully used the New Testament strategy of building the church with small groups for nearly thirty years. DCFI started as a youth ministry in the late 1970s that targeted unchurched youth in southcentral Pennsylvania. The first DOVE Church grew out of the ensuing need for a flexible New Testament-style church that could assist these new believers and grew into a church of more than 2,000 people. Today, the DCFI family consists of cell-based congregations and house churches that network throughout the United States, Central and South America, the Caribbean, Canada, Europe, Africa, Asia, and the South Pacific.

**Contact information for seminars
and speaking engagements:**
Larry Kreider, International Director, DCFI
11 Toll Gate Road, Lititz, PA 17543
Tel: 717-627-1996   Fax: 717-627-4004
www.dcfi.org
LarryK@dcfi.org

Sam Smucker is the senior pastor of The Worship Center, a thriving church family in Lancaster, Pennsylvania. He is a graduate of Rhema Bible Training Center in Tulsa, Oklahoma, and attended Pittsburgh School of the Bible. In 1977, he felt led of the Lord to return to his hometown and pastor a new congregation of 27 people which has since grown to approximately 2,000 people. The Worship Center offers a variety of ministries to minister to all ages. The Word of God is a priority because it is the foundation and source of life. Relationships are also an intricate and life-giving part of this church family, whether through relating to one another in small groups, during events and activities or connecting with God through worship and prayer. The Worship Center also reaches into over 100 countries through their mission's emphasis.

**Contact information for seminars
and speaking engagements:**
Sam Smucker, Senior Pastor, The Worship Center
2384 New Holland Pike, Lancaster, PA 17601
Tele: 717.656.4271   Fax: 717.656.4391
www.worshipcenter.org
pastorsam@worshipcenter.org

Other Resources

Building Your Personal House of Prayer

The Master's plan for daily prayer. Unlocks twelve unique rooms found in the Lord's Prayer. This book will change your prayer life forever! Gives practical steps to immediately improve how you pray. Includes small group outlines and questions. *by Larry Kreider, 254 pages:* **$14.99**

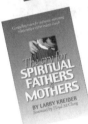

The Cry for Spiritual Fathers and Mothers

The Book Returning to the biblical truth of spiritual parenting so believers are not left fatherless and disconnected. How loving, seasoned spiritual fathers and mothers help spiritual children reach their full potential in Christ. *by Larry Kreider, 186 pages:* **$11.95**

Audio Set of six topics. *Six CD Set:* **$29.00**

You can hear God's voice every day!

Discover how God's voice becomes familiar to you as you develop a loving relationship with him. Take 30 days, reading a chapter a day, to explore 30 of the many ways God speaks. Use as a personal devotional or go through this material with your small group or congregation. *by Larry Kreider, 224 pages:* **$14.99**

Hearing God Audio Book For your home or car. Read by author Larry Kreider on a four CD set: **$24.99**

House To House Publications
Call 800.848.5892
www.dcfi.org   *email: info@dcfi.org*